WHAT NOW?

WHAT NOW?

An introduction to living life with Jesus at the centre

Betsy de Thierry

Terra Nova Publications

First published by Terra Nova Publications 2005

Published in Great Britain by
Terra Nova Publications
PO Box 2400, Bradford on Avon, Wiltshire BA15 2YN

Cover design by Immersive Projects

ISBN 1 90194 936 2

Printed in Great Britain
by Bookmarque Ltd, Croydon.

Contents

The purpose of this book....

*This little book has been written out of a passion to see people live
phenomenal lives, centred on Jesus, where they can begin to taste
heaven on earth. It is designed to introduce, as simply as possible,
how to practically start to live putting Jesus in the centre of your life.
I believe that this is the only way to live 'life in all its fullness'.
It has been one of my major frustrations in life to see people who
want to connect with Jesus losing their natural hunger when they
attempt to wade through intellectual, theological books
(which are great to read once you've established a relationship with Jesus,
but which can be somewhat overwhelming otherwise).
This book is aimed at people who are curious, or beginning to
be hungry to connect with our awesome God
and live life impacted by Him, His love and power.
So read away, and get living the best, most exciting, adventurous,
phenomenal life that you could lead, with Jesus in the centre!*

Thanks

*Thanks to Andrew, my best friend,
my best critic and biggest fan.*

*Thanks to Josh, Ben and Jonah for being the best kids ever!
May you always have Jesus right in the centre of your lives.*

*Thanks to Dad and Mum
for introducing me to Jesus.*

*Thanks to Freedom Centre, Bath
for being the best church ever!*

*Thanks to Christian City Church
for being an awesome, Jesus centred movement
that we are so proud to be a part of.*

1

STARTING A NEW LIFE WITH JESUS

Hi! The main purpose of this book is to help you as you start on this new journey with Jesus. My assumption is that you have either just heard that living with Jesus is exciting, awesome and relevant and you want to know more, or you are just checking out what is happening to a friend of yours who has just decided to follow Jesus (and you want to make sure that she or he is not just going weird), or you have just recently made a decision yourself to give your life to Jesus. Whoever you are, I hope that this book helps to facilitate you connecting with God and the purposes that He has for your life!

Many people believe they are already Christians because they were born in a 'Christian country' or were christened as a child. Even more people assume that they are Christians because they believe in Jesus and think that He was a great guy. Believing in Jesus and all that He said and did is far more awesome than anyone looking on can imagine, and has far more incredible implications for life than you can think possible! This book is going to look at what becoming a Christian really is all about. The Bible makes it clear that the main thing to do to start a relationship with Jesus is to believe, and I want to explain a bit more about that word.

The word 'believe'

Let me tell you an old story about a tightrope walker called Blondin. In 1860 he strung a tightrope across Niagara Falls. Then, in front of ten thousand screaming people, he inched his way from the Canadian side of the Falls to the American side. When he got there, the whole crowd began shouting his name: "Blondin! Blondin!"

Finally he raised his arms, quietened the crowd, and shouted, "I am Blondin! Do you believe in me?"

The crowd shouted back, "We believe, we believe!"

Again he quietened the crowd, and once more he shouted to them, "I am going to carry someone on my back. Do you believe I can do that?"

The crowd yelled enthusiastically, "We believe, we believe!"

He quietened them one more time as he asked them, "Who will be that person?" There was silence – uncomfortable silence – until one person stepped out of the crowd. He then climbed on Blondin's back and spent the next three hours or so inching his way across the rope.

The point of the story is clear: ten thousand people shouted 'we believe', but only one person believed to the point of giving over his life and making a commitment. Believing is not just about agreeing with the facts —it is about making a commitment.

There are many people who believe the facts about Jesus but who do not want Him to affect their lives. That is not being a follower of Jesus! Becoming a Christian, deciding to follow Jesus, or choosing to become a disciple of His, however you want to describe it, is all about allowing Jesus into your life. It is about giving Him your life, recognising that He knows you more than you know yourself, and that He knows the best way for you. It is about moving Jesus into the centre of your life!

Jesus' commitment to you!

That is not an easy step if you do not really take hold of the fact that Jesus is passionately, overwhelmingly and consistently in love with YOU! You could not give someone you cannot see that much influence in your life unless you know beyond doubt that He loves you and is unchanging. It would be no good if He changed His mind just because you feel or look different one day! He is committed to your understanding this immense love, and living in the freedom of knowing it more and more. Nor would it be a good thing if, while knowing He loves you, that was just some 'mystery of the depths' that you could never really understand at all. Jesus wants you to *know* just how much He knows about you, loves you and adores you. He wants you to *know* His love so much that His Holy Spirit has written a book to help you understand this love in your mind. As you spend time with Him and ask Him – at any time of the day or night – to show you His love, He will do that, so that, increasingly, you can understand in your heart. Understanding His love will totally change the way you live your life and the way you feel about life. It is a beautiful thing!

Jesus died on the cross as the ultimate declaration of love for us. He then rose again and demonstrated His power as the totally undefeated Creator. He left us His Holy Spirit so that we can know today His presence, comfort, peace, wisdom and hope. The best thing about all of this is that if you were the only person in the world He would have died for you —just for you. The Bible makes it so clear that He knows you intimately and loves you. It says that, 'while we were still sinners Christ died for us.' He saw us, all messed up on the inside, and chose to die for us. It is so beautiful to know that Jesus knows all the parts of our heart that no one else knows, and He still calls to you and me. He longs for you to know that He sees you and loves you! The Bible tells us that Jesus knows your name and how many hairs are on your head (which is not many to count if you are my husband!) He knows your thoughts, and when you go out and come in. He knew you before you were formed in your mother's womb, and chose for you to be in existence, even if your parents did not —even if you were an 'accident' or seemed to be unplanned, because God planned the day you were conceived, the day you were born, and the angels celebrated you! The day you chose (or choose) to follow Jesus and give your life to Him, the angels have a party —just for you! You are not just a part of a big crowd. You cannot hide behind someone taller, more clever, confident or holy. God chose you; He is calling your name, and He knows you and loves you. Now do you know why we feel so blessed? Jesus knows us and loves us, and that is enough to make anyone feel blessed to be alive, no matter what circumstances they face.

Jesus and God
At this point it needs to be made clear that when we talk about Jesus we really mean 'God' and 'Jesus', because they are one! Jesus is truly God and truly man. Now that sounds really rather complicated! How is it that the Father, the Holy Spirit and Jesus are one? I have no idea how, but I know it is true! It is the mystery of the Trinity. Jesus said, 'I and My Father are one.' So when we mention Jesus we also mean God, and vice versa!

Created to have a relationship with God
It is important to understand how things were meant to be when God created the world. We read in the book of Genesis (at the beginning of the Bible) about the Garden of Eden, where God walked with Adam and Eve in the cool of the day. That sounds to me like the most amazing thing. How many questions we would have liked to ask; how secure and loved we would have felt, walking and talking with God. Then we learn that Adam and Eve messed up by choosing to disobey the instructions that they were given, and things became different. God still wants us to have that kind of relationship with Himself, where we walk and talk with Him; and because we were designed to live like that, life will never work as well without it. People clearly can live without God and be successful, happy and content, but as they are actually not living as they are created to live, they do not know the half of it! Life can only be known in all its fullness when God is in the centre of it.

10

Jesus hated religion

It has to be said at this point that God hates religion! Having a relationship with Jesus is absolutely nothing to do with religion! Religion is that odd set of rules, meaningless repetition and formula which implies that you have to act in a certain way. Now clearly God wants to transform us to become more like Him, and our behaviour will change as we let Him impact our lives with His life. However, God does not want us to become all odd, weird, intense, and unable to talk and relate to people normally! God loves who you are and He loves to look at His people and see diversity. There are some subcultures of Christianity where people have had real and beautiful revelations of God but then are taught that, to truly belong, the girls need to be quiet, docile and wear a whole lot of pearls and frilly dresses, and the guys have to be very serious and look anxious about the end of the world! Clearly this is weird and religious, and is nothing to do with what Jesus wants to do!

In the book of Amos, the writer expresses God's passion as He looks at His people: 'I hate, I despise your feast days, And I do not savour your sacred assemblies.' God does not enjoy solemn, religious ceremonies where people are not being honest. God wants real relationship, not empty solemn ritual. Isn't that great? The church needs to understand this urgently as it seeks to represent the King of kings. God wants to impact the real us! Whoever God made you to be, He just wants to improve, blossom and refine that, and not mould us to all look the same, with bland personalities and strange communication habits! As we all let Jesus impact our lives we will look more and more different, and people will comment on things like our confidence, peace, joy, love and energy, and they will want to know why we have a look in our eyes that looks really alive. That is the reaction to expect if we are letting Jesus into the depths of our lives.

Jesus being the centre of one layer at a time!

So the plan is that when you 'become a Christian' you learn to trust Jesus and believe in Him more and more every day.

The more you understand Him, the more you want to give Him your life. You see, when we say that we 'give Jesus our lives' that is really a statement of what we want to do. Lives, however, are a little complicated, as there are many layers and complex thoughts. I see our lives a little like a house with hundreds of rooms. We are not even aware of what is in half the rooms unless we walk into them. The rooms are sections of our lives; so, for example, one room could be our present relationship with a friend; another room the memories of that relationship, which are great; another room the less great memories; and maybe another room the painful memories where they hurt you intentionally or by a mistake. That is four rooms over one friend. That is a big house. We say to Jesus we want Him to have our whole house and run it Himself with Him in the centre – and, boy, we mean it completely – but it is only as we go through life that God shows us a room and says, 'Well, what about that one then?' It is at that moment we have a choice to give it to Him, slam it shut, or just keep God out of that room! As we pray, spend time with Jesus, and understand Him more, we realise that Jesus wants to bring healing, clear out some stuff, and make each room work really well by showing us His perspective. Does that make sense? So none of us has really got all our rooms totally perfect, as we are creating new rooms all the time anyway; but our desire is that we seek to have every area and section of our life, every single little bit, saturated by Jesus' love, perspective, forgiveness, holiness, healing and presence. That is giving our lives to Jesus and following Him. That is being a Christian.

Who is Jesus?

The best thing to do before anything else is to find out as much as you can about Jesus. Get hold of the Bible (most churches will give you one!) and read the books that are the stories about Jesus. These are Matthew, Mark, Luke and John. It is only as we read about Him and hear other people talking about Him working in their lives that we want to give Him more and more of our lives. To know He is powerful is great, but to know He is powerful when you really need a miracle is more than great —it is awesome. To know that Jesus is patient is great, but to know when you keep messing up that He is patient with *you* is life-changing. To know that Jesus knows your thoughts and innermost life is great, but when everyone, everywhere, seems to misunderstand you and let you down, it becomes totally safe and full of hope and life that He knows and understands.

Let me give you a taster. If you have just (or are really thinking about) beginning a lifetime of commitment to Jesus and God, let me just briefly tell you a little bit about Him. Please do not think that Jesus is some meek and mild, meagre, boring guy who wears a nightie. Jesus is the most phenomenal, powerful, exceptional, awesome person —who we can learn to walk with all our life!

He protects us (Psalm 91)
He is our guide (Psalm 23)
He is our comforter (2 Corinthians 1:3–4)
He brings peace that the world does not understand
(John 14:27)
He is patient (Matthew 18:26–27)
He loves us (John 3:16)
He is our Father (Romans 8:15)
He is compassionate (2 Corinthians 1:3)
He is faithful (Isaiah 49:7)
He provides for us (Matthew 6:33)
He is our rock (Psalm 18:2)
He is the healer (Matthew 8:16)
He is our strength (Psalm 28:7)
He is our refuge (Psalm 46:1)
He forgives us (1 John 1:9)
He wants to set us free from fear (Psalm 118:5–9)
He wants to bind up the brokenhearted (Isaiah 61:1)
He wants to answer our prayers (James 5:16–18)
He delights to show mercy (Micah 7:18)
He wants to give us life in all its fullness (John 10:10)

The list could go on and on and on! He is amazing, wonderful and beautiful. I pray that you will want to know Him. It is not the same to know about someone as it is to know someone.

Knowing Jesus is finding reality

The world tells us that it is not normal to be a passionate follower of Jesus. In fact, many people in the world believe that passion can only be expressed in sports, entertainment and love. The fact is that we know that God created us to live with Him, and being in a relationship with the Creator of the world – and the One who is Love – is unlikely to be boring, mediocre or dull! It is the most wonderful, amazing adventure, where we find what truth and reality really are. Being in the presence of Jesus is where we can find love, peace, joy, and life in all its fullness.

Questions to think about

1. Have I decided to follow Jesus and make a decision to give Him my life?
2. Have I told someone that I have done that?
3. Have I understood, at least a little bit, why Jesus died on the cross for me?
4. Have I started to understand just how much Jesus loves me?
5. Have I decided to give Jesus each layer of my life as He shows me?
6. Have I begun to learn more and more about Jesus?

2

PRAYER —
SPENDING TIME WITH JESUS

The importance of communication

All our relationships work best if we talk and listen. Have you ever managed to remain friends with someone who you never talk to or listen to? Communication is fuel for any relationship, and 'becoming a Christian' is all about starting to have a real, deep friendship with Jesus. The only way to do that is to spend time with Him!

'But I can't see Him', you cry out! This is actually a very good point. It is no good pretending; it would be easier if we could see Him and run up to Him and kneel down or have a hug. Wouldn't that be great! But we are going to have to wait for heaven for that, so it is all about learning the best way for you to build your relationship with Jesus now!

Now the funny thing is that in my marriage (I have been married for over ten years) no one has ever tried to suggest the best way of us communicating. We worked it out for ourselves —and, as it happens, we talk best when we are in coffee shops or in the car. That is us, and it probably is not the same for you. You see, in a relationship if you both want to spend time together, then you will. It is just working out, through trial and error, where and when is the best way of doing it. It is actually the same in your walk with Jesus — working out the best way for you to spend time with Him.

Where do I pray?

For some people the best place to pray is at home, in your room, on your knees. For others it is while walking in the hills and open country (that's my husband!), and for others it can be pacing up and down the sitting room floor with loud worship music.

Actually, it does not matter where you pray, although, just as with any relationship, there are sensible boundaries. Spending time with Jesus while you watch television, or playing music with lyrics that He would not like, is not conducive to a loving relationship. Your spouse or friend would feel undervalued were you to treat them like that. It is important that, wherever you pray, you know that Jesus is the main focus, and you feel able to think, feel, connect, express yourself, talk and listen. Jesus, warning of those He called 'the hypocrites' who loved to be seen by others praying, explained how to pray in such a way that you are not drawing attention to yourself and showing off. He says,

> "But when you pray, go into your room, and when you have shut your door, pray to your Father who is in the secret place...."
>
> *Matthew 6:6a*

What do I talk about?

Just as with other relationships, there are times when it is really good to have some special time (like a date) with Jesus, and there are times when it is good to just hang out together; and the rest of the time it is awesome just to be aware of His presence —that is not like any other friendship! On dates with Him, you give Him your undivided attention and are intimate with Him. By that I mean that you don't just talk about the weather and events, but feelings; deep stuff that you cannot say when you are in a rush or in a supermarket queue. It is taking the time to wait for Him to reveal Himself. Just sitting in His presence and 'waiting' on Him is key to knowing His power, equipping, revelation and love in your life. When you wait, you engage all your senses to focus and long for Jesus; and then you settle yourself to be patient and enjoy the time. The Bible says this:

> But those who wait on the LORD
> Shall renew their strength
>
> *Isaiah 40:31*

> For You are the God of my salvation;
> On You I wait all the day.
>
> *Psalm 25:5*

It is great to tell Him how you felt and feel about stuff; your worries, fears, excitements, and concerns. That is how Jesus becomes a part of every area of your life. It is at these special times with Jesus that you can allow Him to fill you up with His presence, or sit quietly and sense His peace or power. It is all about taking time with Him and not rushing it.

The rest of the time, when you are just doing life with Jesus, it is great to chat to Him about anything and everything. Sometimes you can't chat, as you are concentrating on other stuff, like your job or kids, but there is always time at some point in the day to say 'Hi!' It is so great to remember Jesus in the day and involve Him in stuff! The amazing thing is that He loves to know all about the small details of our lives, which seem as though they would be so insignificant – or so we think – to the ruler of the whole universe; but this is one of the overwhelming things about Jesus —He loves to listen. He listens to millions of people all at the same time! David, who wrote most of Psalms (a big book in the middle of the Bible that is well worth reading a.s.a.p!) was amazed at this, commenting: 'What is man that You are mindful of him...?' (Psalm 8:4); and, 'For there is not a word on my tongue, But behold, O LORD, You know it altogether' (Psalm 139:4).

So, you ask, why on earth should I bother talking to Him if He knows all my thoughts anyway? The reason is that He wants you to tell Him anyway. He loves to listen to you. That is what a relationship is like. Often people around me who know me well will know what I am going to say in certain situations, but it would be very odd if I did not bother talking, and vice versa.

How do we worship?
We were made to worship God. Worship is the act of giving worth to something or someone. If we do not worship God, then, because we were made to worship, we will find some outlet for that need in our hearts. We cannot stop worshipping something, because God has given us a spirit that naturally craves to worship, and for many people they worship money, football, popularity, success or themselves. As we worship God, our spirit connects with His and becomes alive, and the presence of God will increase in our world. This is not a solemn, religious experience, but a life-giving, exciting connection. One way we express our worship is through music. This helps us to connect our minds and emotions with our spirit. As we spend time praying, it is helpful to use music to connect to God. There is power in praise; praise creates an environment that welcomes God; praise proclaims truth; praise opens up your spirit to the King of kings. The book of the prophet Isaiah teaches us that a major characteristic of God's people will be praise. So get praising! Get worshipping the King of kings, and experience the beauty and power of His presence.

What about praying for other people and for things to happen?
Of course the amazing thing about prayer is that talking to God is not like talking to anyone else. He is the maker of the universe, and is all powerful. It says in the Bible that '...with God all things are possible' (Matthew 19:26). He is actually waiting for His children to ask Him for things. It teaches us also that we are to pray and not give up. (See Luke 11:8). The big thing is actually to remember to be specific! The Bible shows us that specific requests are generally better than vague ones. If you pray that you want your family to be blessed, you can know that God's will is to do that —but He loves you to be as specific as you can about what is needed.

The Bible teaches us clearly that God wants us to ask Him for things, and to be persistent in asking. So what kind of things are we meant to ask for? Things that our Father, who adores us, wants for us too! He wants us to pray for more of Him in our lives; to be more like Jesus; to love people more and hear Him more. He wants us to pray for individuals we know to have a revelation of Jesus and to give their lives to Him. He wants us to pray for people to be healed; to know His love, guidance, wisdom, power, compassion. He wants us to pray for His will to be accomplished and His way to be followed everywhere. He wants us to pray for help, wisdom and guidance in every part of our lives. Jesus wants to be involved in all parts of our lives!

Jesus teaches us how to pray

Jesus gives us a great guide for prayer. This is a prayer that so many people used to learn off by heart and pray in school assemblies without any heart connection to Jesus. It is actually an awesome insight into how to pray powerfully, if it is used as a springboard. The prayer is written in Matthew 6:9 –15. Let's look at what Jesus was teaching us about prayer. The prayer starts:

Our Father in heaven, hallowed be Your name.
This means that it is important to come to Jesus knowing that He perfectly reveals the nature of our Father who loves, cares and knows us. He protects, nurtures and loves us, and He is in heaven, seated above all things. He is amazing, and worthy to be praised. It is important to praise Him for who He is. Our whole perspective on life changes as we begin to look at God and who He is! Praise is powerful! The prayer continues:

Your kingdom come. Your will be done on earth as it is in heaven.
Here, you are praying for more people to give their lives to Jesus; and for those of us who have done that to do more

of Jesus' works in this earth, and so expand His kingdom —which is everywhere He reigns. Basically, it is declaring that you want to see more of everything that Jesus wants done in this earth as it is in heaven, and you are prepared to be an active part of that, as He tells you how to live and what to say and do. God already reigns in heaven and He wants His world back, through people desiring that this will happen. Heaven is a great place, and God wants this earth to be a great place too. The prayer goes on:

Give us this day our daily bread.
This means that we are meant to pray that God will provide for us everything we need. God is our Father who promises to give us everything we need, and we need to continually remember that all things belong to Him, and He is the source of all good things! Miracles of provision are only a persistent prayer away!

And forgive us our debts, as we forgive our debtors.
['Debts' can also be translated 'sins'.]
We are to ask Jesus to forgive us for anything that we have done to hurt Him. We take time to ask Him to show us any sin or wrongdoing, knowing that He does forgive us and 'cleanse us from all unrighteousness'. He asks us to forgive all the people who have hurt us, too, which can be harder! The deal is that if Jesus forgives us, then what right do we have to withhold forgiveness from anyone else? We are all 'sinners saved by grace'. Forgiving others is not a feeling, it is a choice —which we then pray that God will help us to keep choosing. There will always be people who will hurt us, as that is part of the reality of relationships, but God is the only judge. If we decide to withhold forgiveness, then there is a root of bitterness and anger which can eat away at our insides. Even if we think we can handle it, ironically, unforgiveness usually causes us to suffer somehow. Jesus teaches us to let go and allow Him to heal our hurts.

And do not lead us into temptation, but deliver us from the evil one.

This means that we are consciously choosing to keep away from activities, places and things that could tempt us to go against God's way. We pray that He gives us the courage and strength to stay away from these things and keep us from temptation. It could be that we are tempted to steal, lie, bitch about someone, gossip, slander, be selfish, etc. If we find ourselves more prone to do these things in certain places, then we need to avoid those places. We also pray that we will be protected from the schemes of the devil (who Jesus has already defeated, but who we need to resist and overcome in our own lives, in our own little areas).

John put it clearly when he wrote, '...He who is in you is greater than he who is in the world' (1 John 4:4b). That means that Jesus is infinitely greater than the devil, but it is wise to be on our guard against any of the tricks of Satan designed to trip us up, by being sensible with where we go and who we hang out with.

For Yours is the kingdom and the power and the glory forever. Amen.

This helps us to remember how awesome God is. We should take time to dwell on how everything belongs to Him: all power, all the glory and all the world belongs to Him. This puts everything in our world, and all our prayers about ourselves and our needs, back into the perspective that He is powerful enough to do everything.

So those are the kinds of things that Jesus wants us to pray about, but it is not meant to be prayed line after line without thinking. It is meant to be used as a guide to how to pray and what to pray. Jesus wants us to pray out of the depths of our hearts rather than as a formula.

How on earth do I listen to someone I cannot see?
Just like in an ordinary human relationship, it is important to take the time to *listen* to Jesus. Prayer is not just a shopping list of requests but a relationship. Therefore prayer is talking and listening. Not very often does God speak with an audible voice, although He does do so very occasionally. He usually speaks to us in our thoughts, dreams, through other people, impressions, and, of course, through the Bible. So the big question for most people is: How do I know whether it is God talking to me, or me making it up? That is where getting to know the Bible is really important, because the Bible is always the plumbline. If you feel that God has ever said anything that is in any way contrary to the Bible, then it is not God speaking to you at all. The Bible is God's unchanging word —and it is more important than any other words that we think God might have said. It is really important to get that straight before going anywhere else, otherwise you will get really confused!

Dreams
God does often speak through dreams. Throughout the Bible He has spoken to people in this way (Joseph, Daniel, John and so on), and for some of us it seems to be a great time for God to speak to us when we're still and quiet. The first dream I ever had that I knew was from God (once the event happened) was when I was seven. I was starting a new school and was very nervous about making new friends. The night before I started the school, I had a dream of a girl with dark hair in bunches and freckles on her face. In the morning I told my parents at breakfast, and they said that maybe Jesus was telling me that she could be my new friend. Well, that morning I walked into my new classroom, and the desk that was free to sit at was next to a girl with dark hair in bunches, and she had freckles on her face. Her name was Tanya, and she was my best friend while I was at that school. How cool is that! God has often given us significant dreams that have meant something to us after the event, which beautifully reminded us that God knew and He was

in control. Sometimes we have had dreams that we did not understand, but we have had a sense that God was trying to talk to us. If that happens, we chat to other people in case they have any interpretation idea, or we just wait and pray. If we forget about it, then the dream was probably not from God anyway. We find that He helps us to remember dreams that are messages from Jesus, and we forget the others.

Thoughts

In another chapter I talk about our thought life, because sorting out our thoughts is a massive part of being a follower of Jesus. However, to introduce very briefly here the subject of hearing Jesus inwardly, we need to remember certain things. In my experience, He very often speaks to me in my mind by reminding me of a Bible verse or a worship song. The words seem to come into my mind almost randomly, maybe when I first wake up in the morning or when I am thinking about some matter. Then I know it is from God because it is His word, and it seemed to 'pop' into my head! He does speak to me using other words, and they always sound like God as they just confirm what I knew about God, but it is wisdom applied to my actual circumstances there and then. If any thoughts do not agree with the Bible – even if they seem to say 'this is what God says!' – they really are not from Him. The whole thing of listening to God definitely gets easier the more you know His character and the Bible. Learning to develop the skill of listening to God comes with practice, and it is good to remember that Jesus actually wants us to hear Him.

Other people

Sometimes God uses other people to speak His words to us. How do we know if they are from God? Very often when people say stuff to me that they feel is from God, I get a kind of strong beating in my heart and a kind of 'Wow, that's me' feeling. Sometimes, it is just nice words that are probably great but not 'from God', but that is OK. As usual, if it does not say what is in the Bible then it is not from God. For example, He would never tell us to kill ourselves or steal. We are meant to be God's family, so it is wonderful when other people do hear God and share with us what they think He is saying, and it is our responsibility to weigh up if it feels right in our spirit or not.

Praying regularly

So, in conclusion, start praying. Do not worry about how to do it and if it is the right way or not —just get on and pray! Enjoy your relationship with Jesus. Connect your heart to His. It is a beautiful thing.

Remember that prayer changes lives —our own, and others' lives, too.

> The effective, fervent prayer of a righteous man avails much.
>
> *James 5:16b*

Read the verses which follow that one, about how miracles can happen when people pray. Go for it!

Questions to think about

1. Where is the best place for me to really focus on Jesus —talking to Him and spending time with Him?
2. What time of day is best for me?
3. Do I find it easy to include Jesus in my day?
4. Do I find it exciting to pray for other people?
5. Have I started to practise listening to God?

3

CHURCH:
THE HOUSE OF GOD

The church is the most astounding concept; it is designed to be a greenhouse full of the presence of God. It is a place to give, a place to grow, a place to be connected, rooted and belong. It is not the building but the people; a bunch of ordinary people who want to know the extraordinary God —people from different backgrounds and cultures, with different struggles and passions, all meeting together, curious or passionate, desperate or excited about one person, Jesus.

To build God's church is our primary cause in this earth. We have to get hold of the fact that it is not an optional extra. In the Book of Revelation, God calls the church His bride. If you went to a wedding feast and slandered the bride it would be offensive! To decide not to be passionate about the church is offensive to God.

The church is about connecting to God and to each other.
The church is not just about Sunday services.
The church is all about Jesus.
The church is the most amazing, phenomenal, awesome and beautiful place, where the presence of God inspires and refreshes your soul. In the church you will find your destiny.

Our attitude to God's house

Many people are not passionate about God's house because their approach is all wrong, People have fundamentally misunderstood the purpose and role of the church in this world, and it has caused them to feel disillusioned and confused. They are missing out on all the joy, honour and excitement that we experience. For many people, going to church is just another thing that has to be 'done' in the list of responsibilities and demands in their stressed and exhausting life. It is just another place that demands time, energy and money that they feel they have to sacrifice out of a sense of duty.

The thing is that Jesus' passion for His house was demonstrated quite spectacularly, and it is this reaction that should help us begin a journey to let Him impact our hearts with a similar passion. Jesus sees people using the temple as a market place, and He reacted with amazing anger as He overturned tables and drove the people and animals out.

And He said to those who sold doves, "Take these things away! Do not make My Father's house a house of merchandise!" Then His disciples remembered that it was written, "Zeal for Your house has eaten Me up."

John 2:16

We need to be people who understand the purpose of God's house and are driven by a righteous passion to see it free from religion and death and restored to being a place full of His presence, plans and power.

Our expectation

As we think about church, there should be an excitement rising in us because we anticipate all the awesome things that happen as God's people meet together to praise Him. We should expect to see the power of God touch people's lives, healing bodies, hearts and relationships. We should come to church meetings excited about being in the powerful presence of God, and experiencing His life, energy, strength and wisdom being poured into our hearts. The church meeting together is the place to go to see phenomenal miracles and lives being restored!

Looking at five descriptions of church

The church can be described using different pictures and words, none of which on its own would adequately depict all that God intended it to be for His people. There are five descriptions I want to look at in more detail now, so that you can grasp just how phenomenal the church really is.

1. The church as a family

Love for each other

Jesus commanded His followers to love each other! Jesus says, "This is My commandment, that you love one another as I have loved you" (John 15:12). That is a fairly major thing to ask!

The church is not just another club that you can join, like the golf club or the book club. It is a family that you become a part of, where God is the Dad who loves all His children. The word 'family' immediately indicates the level of commitment that we suddenly have towards each other. We cannot choose to hate each other; we have to love, help and care for each other. Jesus said, "By this all will know that you are My disciples, if you have love for one another" (John 13:35). Love is not a feeling, it is a way of life. Paul wrote,

> Love suffers long and is kind; love does not envy; love does not parade itself, is not puffed up; does not behave rudely, does not seek its own, is not provoked, thinks no evil; does not rejoice in iniquity, but rejoices in the truth; bears all things, believes all things, hopes all things, endures all things. Love never fails.
>
> *1 Corinthians 13:4–8a*

We have to learn to live like this with everyone, not just other people who are following Jesus; but the church should be oozing and bursting with everyone trying to live in this way. It should be the most loving, warm, forgiving, trusting place. That will only happen if everyone wants to live like this and does not just expect everyone else to try while they cannot be bothered! That does not work —think about it!

When the first church started, Paul wrote,

Now all who believed were together, and had all things in common, and sold their possessions and goods, and divided them among all, as anyone had need.

So continuing daily with one accord in the temple, each day, and breaking bread from house to house, they ate their food with gladness and simplicity of heart, praising God and having favour with all the people.

Acts 2:44–47a

Spending time together

A major purpose of the church is that we spend time with each other —encouraging each other, helping each other and enjoying each other! So play is something that we are called to do! We have a little phrase which we use a lot in our church: 'If you laugh together, it's easier to cry together.' This means that if you have fun together it is easier to spend time being honest and vulnerable with each other. People often comment to us when we are out in groups having fun, playing skittles, buying vast amounts of food for parties, etc., that it looks like we are having fun. People often ask us if we are an extended family because we are in groups of people who are different ages who seem to know and trust each other. Our reply is that we are a family, and then we try and explain! The great thing about this family is that we are always growing and expanding. In the very heart of this church family lies an intensely outward looking, welcoming and warm nature. The concept of 'holy huddles', where new people feel awkward, is nothing to do with the nature of this ever expanding, fun, loving, caring and outward looking family!

Dealing with conflict

The church family is made up of millions of people all over the world who all share the same Father; and like a normal family there are sometimes conflicts, disagreements and fallings out. The good news is that this family has a book that teaches us how to work through all these times for the best of everyone: the Bible! Matthew 18 tells us all about how to deal with conflict. Conflict is not the problem. It will happen in a healthy home where people feel that they can be themselves and not just sit passively; but it does matter how you handle it, as that can make, break or strain relationships. The key thing is to first pray about any problem, and try to wait to see what Jesus says about it. Then, if necessary, talk to the person concerned, honestly and with an attitude of wanting the best for them. The important thing is that gossiping, backbiting or bitching is not love but evidence of an unloving heart, and therefore to be avoided Let us be people who are determined to walk through disagreements with maturity and love.

Commitment to each other

Commitment is a really important part of making a church healthy. It is not like a club where you can change membership according to the facilities and deals on at the time. In Psalm 92:13, the psalmist says:

> Those who are planted in the house of the LORD
> shall flourish in the courts of our God.
> They shall still bear fruit in old age;
> They shall be fresh and flourishing,
> To declare that the LORD is upright;
> He is my rock,
> and there is no unrighteousness in Him.

If you continually uprooted your houseplant into a new pot each Sunday, or even yearly, eventually the plant would die. The plant needs to make roots in order to grow and flourish. The same is true of us: if we run away from our church every time we have a disagreement or if we just feel like a change for a while, we are uprooting ourselves. Without roots, it is hard to flourish. If the church down the road suddenly has an exciting time with God, don't run down there, stick at your pot and pray for God to move there (unless the 'pot' has not been 'watered' for years, and then you would be silly to stay. If the horse is dead, then dismount!) If everyone runs to the church that has the latest excitement, then no roots are formed, we have total anarchy, and everyone is treating the house of God as if it were a shopping mall. Oh, and no you cannot belong to two churches. How can you? A plant cannot have two pots. You cannot have two bosses who are different, can you? You can only really be rooted into one church. If you are going to two churches at the moment, then work out which one God wants you to be part of. Which is the one that is feeding you and growing you? That is the one that you are called to be in.

2. The church as a hospital

The church is called to care for those who need care and healing, so there is a side of the church that serves as a 'hospital'.

Physical and emotional healing

The church is also called to be a hospital where people get healed by Jesus. Jesus came to heal the broken hearted and the physically ill, and the church is called to continue His works in this world. Isaiah 61 says:

> The Spirit of the Lord GOD is upon Me,
> Because the LORD has anointed Me
> To preach good tidings to the poor;
> He has sent Me to heal the brokenhearted,
> To proclaim liberty to the captives,
> And the opening of the prison to
> those who are bound....

That prophecy talks about what Jesus would do when He walked on this earth, and therefore what the followers of Jesus are called to do now. Jesus said:

> "...he who believes in Me, the works that I do he will do also; and greater works than these he will do, because I go to My Father."
>
> *John 14:12*

So as we care for each other as a family, we also pray for each other to see healing happen. Sometimes people get healed immediately, and sometimes we have to keep praying until it happens. Sometimes healing does not come, and we have to say we do not understand everything on this earth. What we do know is that we are only here for about eighty years or so, and God sees the bigger picture which we can ask Him about one day. We can be totally assured that He can do anything and wants the best for us.

People supporting each other
Because the church is called to be a 'hospital', in most churches there is opportunity to have someone pray for you at some point in the meeting as you deal with something in your life that God is bringing to the surface. Sunday meetings are also the perfect time to ask someone to pray for you as you live through the difficult stuff that happens in life. The great thing about church is that it is a rare place where everyone recognises that we are all 'sinners saved by grace' who are all working our salvation out with 'fear and trembling'. This basically means that we are all dealing with stuff in our life that needs changing —all the time, until we die! No one is totally and completely perfect. It is not a depressing fact, but a life-giving thing; we recognise that when we are all trying to be like Jesus as our life's goal, we are going to take a while! So it is seen as quite odd if you are all completely sorted and together in every area of your life.

People are not Jesus

It's an amazing thing to have someone standing with you, giving up their time to support you and pray for you, as you move through issues in your life. It is important to remember, though, that it is not them doing the healing. It is all about your relationship with God, and the family just providing some support. It is also really important to remember that it is all about Jesus and trusting Him, because all people, no matter how hard they try, not being perfect will probably make mistakes. They may not say the right thing or may mess up at some point. If you know that people just do that sometimes, it is not such a shock when it happens. Some people end up having a huge faith crisis because they assume that anyone who has known Jesus for longer than them must be nearly perfect, and so they get really hurt when they are not completely faultless.

In churches there are usually counselling teams, listening teams and other people who can provide prayer and support as you work through stuff that arises in your life. It is normal in the house of God to be working through issues, and it is a sign that you recognise God has not finished with you yet.

The hospital wing

The danger in all of this is that people can rather enjoy the navel gazing side of things, and it can feel quite good and even addictive, to be thinking about your inner hurts and pains. Life involves pain, and that cannot be avoided. Most of the time we just get up, press into Jesus, and walk through it. There are seasons to be in what we call 'the hospital wing' of the church where the main thing God seems to be doing in your life is healing pains and dealing with strongholds; but as with any hospital, if your experience of church is mainly as your hospital, you will get spiritual bed sores! God has not designed any of us to spend too many long, concentrated times dealing with pains and memories. We are meant to be running forward. There are times when you need to see a spiritual 'nurse' or 'doctor' (small group leader or pastor) for a session of prayer about an issue, but most of the time you can sort the issue out directly with the Healer Himself by praying and spending time with Him. Occasionally, you may need to spend time in the hospital wing, which merely means that you take every opportunity for prayer (not that most of us don't take every opportunity anyway!) When that season passes (most spiritual operations last a few weeks or months of God healing you, while you spend time worshipping and praying on your own mostly) you are back out there pouring yourself out for others.

You see, the danger is if everyone sees the church as a hospital with one consultant (the leader) there will be massive trolley pile ups everywhere; lots of self pity and grumbling, and none of the works that Jesus told us to do in the great commission being done! Self pity can be very addictive and yet is a crippling disease which causes more people to be locked into captivity than any problem. Self pity stops faith. Without faith we cannot please God and we will not be able to walk into the things that He has for us. Make a decision to stamp out self pity in your life and the lives around you!

3. The church as a school

Clearly one of the roles of the church is to teach people and to facilitate learning.

Formal teaching

The church's role as a school is often obvious because of the preaching and teaching which most people associate with a church meeting. This is great formal teaching, where a few people teach a large crowd about a subject that God wants to reveal to His people. I find it amazing how this works. Think about it: a large group, all of whom are facing different issues and have known or have not known Jesus for different lengths of time, all listening to the same talk and finding that it builds up their inner life. It cannot be too simple for those who have theology degrees or who have been following Jesus for years, but it cannot be too complex for those who are trying to learn who Jesus is. It is all down to the Holy Spirit working and applying it directly to our own lives. It is a beautiful thing to watch. The best way to approach the teaching in church is with a hungry heart that is excited to hear what God wants to say to His people.

Formal discipleship
The word 'disciple' means follower. So the main job of a disciple is to learn about who you are following and what they did. As people who are choosing to become Jesus' disciples, we need to want to be discipled. This can be quite a daunting task when you realise that the Bible is the main book to be studied, understood and lived, as that shows us what Jesus was like and how to be like Him. Therefore it can be great to have some help in understanding it all, and that is where small groups aimed at this can help. Churches often have some form of mentoring system set up for people who are new to following Jesus, which is great. It does not mean that you are thick, stupid or a lower class of follower of Jesus if you ask for help; it shows that you are intelligent, wise and have a great future, as you realise that you do not want to miss any precious pearls.

We love to hang out with people who have been following Jesus for longer than us. We love to grill them for anything we can learn, any revelations they have had, or anything that they want to tell us which could help us. We will never have learned all there is to know about Jesus, and He gives different people different revelations, so we all need each other in the church. There are few limits on a teachable, humble heart!

Informal discipleship
One of the most amazing ways of moving forward in your walk with God is simply being around other people who are following Jesus. When you are around other people who have been walking with Jesus for some time, it is natural to catch some of their revelations of who He is and what He does. It

is not so much that they explain some teaching to you, but more that you see things in their life that you recognise as being like Jesus. It often seems to almost 'rub off on you', and, before you know it, you are acting in the same way. In any friendship groups there will often be people who will wind you up or irritate you as well, and it is actually at that moment that all the teachings about Jesus being loving, patient, kind and forgiving really take on a new meaning. Many people see the 'irritating person' as the person who is hindering their discipleship and learning process, and causing them problems, whereas actually they are there to make sure all the head learning becomes earthed in normal everyday life. It is normal to agree with – and be passionate about – Jesus teaching you to be patient, until you have an annoying person right there in your first small group! Jesus wants to help you to see how your reactions need Him, and you need His strength to change. We cannot change ourselves very effectively by striving, feeling really guilty, or being quiet and still. We change by the power of the Holy Spirit working in our lives as we ask Him to!

'Not by might, nor by power, but by My Spirit,' says the LORD of hosts.

Zechariah 4:6b

Learning by doing

Another really great part of the school side of church is the doing bit. This bit is so often misunderstood and undervalued. Many people believe that learning is all about storing up information in your head, so that you sound intelligent. This is not actually true. Learning is all about translating the stuff that you hear into actions and attitudes and lifestyles.

From James' letter in the New Testament, we learn that faith without actions is dead. (He explained this to Jewish Christians.) Discipleship is about how your life changes to be more like Jesus, and that can take time. It seems to be a very long way between our brains understanding things in part, and then understanding a bit more —and then it reaches our actions and behaviour. So one good way to help you learn is your helping other people. You can join teams of people in the church who are serving. There is something that everyone can do: serve the teas and coffees, give business advice, serve on the kids' teams, encourage someone, make cakes for your small group, babysit, mow someone's lawn, and smile at someone. That is called living out the teachings of Jesus!

4. The church as an army

Not just on the defensive

The church is also called to be an army. The church is a group of people on a mission, who know that they have an enemy, but also know that they are on the winning team. We are a team of people who are trying to help others move from the losing team to the winning team. We are out not just to defend our faith, as if it were some sad fragile flower on the edge of extinction (as so many people seem to think), but to take territory from the enemy, defeat strongholds and see the kingdom of Jesus expanded. Therefore we want to be people who pray long and hard to see our friends and family get to know Jesus and give their lives to Him. We want to be people who stand up for what we believe in, rather than living ashamed of being in the minority. We are determined, definite, gutsy, prepared to take risks, sacrificial, giving, joyful people, all seeking to obey Jesus our commander. Ephesians 6:10–17 describes the 'spiritual armour' to 'wear' as a follower of Jesus.

Finally, my brethren, be strong in the Lord and in the power of His might. Put on the whole armour of God, that you may be able to stand against the wiles of the devil. For we do not wrestle against flesh and blood, but against principalities, against powers, against the rulers of the darkness of this age, against spiritual hosts of wickedness in the heavenly places. Therefore take up the whole armour of God, that you may be able to withstand in the evil day, and having done all, to stand.

Ephesians 6:10–13

Authority structures

The church is not a hierarchical structure with leaders at the top of some ladder removed from the mere paupers at the bottom! The leaders are the greatest servants who serve the troops. However, the troops need to be directed and led by the leaders. Leaders can only lead effectively if the troops (or people in the churches) recognise the authority that God has placed on them, and want to win the battles with the strategies given to those leaders. Each individual follower of Jesus is responsible for their own actions; hears God personally, and has their own personal relationship with Jesus, but also needs to recognise the importance of being accountable and submitted to a leader. The leader needs to be submitted to their leader, and so it goes on, so that people are not just doing 'what is right in their own eyes', as this is one dangerous place to be in. An army does not work if it is full of independent, rebellious, stubborn, unsubmitted people who want to do their own thing on their own. That is anarchy. On the other hand, a leader who is controlling, manipulating, shaming or self seeking is not a godly leader. Find a leader who seems godly, and be submitted to them so that we can all run together in one direction to see amazing things happen in the building of God's house.

A different kind of army

The different thing about this army is that its motive is love and compassion. The hallmark of the army is joy; not happiness, which is based on good happenings and circumstances, but joy, which is a God thing, a deep down knowledge of Jesus' love and of His purposes being fulfilled. It is an exciting place to be.

5. The church as the bride of Christ

Jesus' love for His church

The church is also described as the bride of Christ, with Jesus as the bridegroom. This image helps us understand how much Jesus loves the church. In an age when many have decided that it is easier only to have relationships with people they already get on with, so that they do not have to work through all the pain of difference, the church as a concept is becoming less popular. But the Bible clearly tells us not to give up meeting together (See Hebrews 10:25). Sometimes it is easier to hang out with people who you naturally love, but that certainly is not a refining place, so ultimately it will not be such a place of blessing. Jesus describes His intense love for His church. He wants His church to be a place of unity, of sacrifice and practical love for each other. The concept of church is awesome, and the enemy will try and get people to fall away from this place of safety, by sowing seeds of doubt when relationships seem to be struggling or the preacher seems uninspiring. It is not about feelings but about commitment to building God's house to be a place of love and beauty. You are a living stone! So be built upon, be available, find your right place to be. A living stone can bear weight, and knows that it is a part of the wall. Peter wrote, '...you also, as living stones, are being built up a spiritual house....' (See 1 Peter 2:5.)

Decide to be a person who is a passionate, alive stone who knows your role and loves to be a part of His bride. Be protective and defensive of God's house. Let passion for how it should be consume you, and then pray, initiate, fight, love, serve, submit, and honour others above yourselves!

Questions to think about

1. Do I understand what the church is meant to be?
2. How do I care for other people in the church?
3. Am I planted and rooted in one church that is my family?
4. Do I understand my role in helping to build God's house?

4

READING THE BIBLE

Why read the Bible?
The Bible is an extremely popular book. It is estimated that nearly 1,250,000 Bibles and Testaments are sold in the UK each year. It is the most amazing book, and is central to the lives of people who are following Jesus. It is made up of 66 individual books: 27 in the New Testament and 39 in the Old Testament, the majority of which spans about 1800 years of history. The Bible is read by different people who are from totally diverse walks of life. Most people who read it recognise that it is a book full of wisdom, great stories, poems, phenomenal literature, and stories about history and about Jesus.

For Christians – people who want to put Jesus in the centre of their lives – the Bible is more than just another great book. In the Bible, Paul wrote about it, calling it 'Scripture':

> All Scripture is given by inspiration of God, and is profitable for doctrine, for reproof, for correction, for instruction in righteousness, that the man of God may be complete, thoroughly equipped for every good work.
>
> *2 Timothy 3:16–17*

This means that we believe that the Bible is God speaking to us. Of course He used humans to write it, but we believe that, unlike any other book, it is completely inspired by God. Therefore if we want to follow God and Jesus, then reading the Bible to know about Him is the obvious thing to do.

The Bible can change our lives

> Blessed is the man
> Who walks not in the counsel of the ungodly,
> Nor stands in the path of sinners,
> Nor sits in the seat of the scornful;
> But his delight is in the law of the LORD,
> And in His law he meditates day and night.
> He shall be like a tree
> Planted by the rivers of water,
> That brings forth its fruit in its season,
> Whose leaf also shall not wither;
> And whatever he does shall prosper.
>
> *Psalm 1:1–3*

That amazing passage teaches us to think about the words of the Bible all the time —because they are life giving. The words of the Bible tell us to live life in a very different way from living in the 'wisdom' of people who do not know God. The Bible will help us know how to live life God's way, and how to live with Jesus at the centre. This way of life is full of blessing, fruitfulness and strength.

The word of God

The thing about the word of God is the power in it. These days people very rarely realise how much power all words have. Everyone says things they do not mean, like, 'I'm dying for a coffee!' and, 'If you do that, I'll kill you.' Words like that are spoken all the time and not truly meant, because people do not know that words have power to create or destroy. God created the world by the power of His spoken word. We do not read about Him mixing potions to make light, do we? He

40

just said (In Genesis 1), "Let there be light", and there was light! Now those words were powerful! If we realize that in the same chapter it says that we are created in God's image, then we see why all our words have power too. (That is why prayer is so powerful.) If we keep saying that everything is terrible and nothing ever goes well for us, then that often becomes true; we so believe what we say that we would not notice the small things that go right anyway! We build our world by what we speak. That does not mean that we cannot be honest and say that we are struggling, if we are. That would be stupid and fake. It is about understanding that we have been given the power to change situations. If things are going wrong, I keep my eyes on God, reminding myself of the truth of God's power and love, without allowing myself to get buried in any words of negativity which can lead to lack of faith or just feeling depressed.

As the Bible is the actual word of God, then, so its words are very powerful. In Ephesians chapter 6, tools that we should use to help keep Jesus in the centre of our lives when we are fighting daily battles are termed 'the armour of God'. The battles we fight can often be our natural desires warring against wanting to live for God; there are battles in our mind to live a holy life, choosing to listen to God and His truth —not the lies of the enemy and the confusion of the world's 'wisdom'. The main weapon God has given us is the word of God, which is described in this list of tools as the 'sword of the Spirit'. That means we can fight thoughts, accusations and so on (not with real swords, clearly!) with Bible verses, because they are powerful. We can read about Jesus doing exactly this when He was being tempted on the mountain, just before He was baptised.

Where did the Bible come from?
Some parts of the Bible came from oral tradition, by which is meant stories people passed down from generation to generation. That is a skill which has almost been lost in much of the modern world, because of the impact of visual media and literature, but it remains alive in many

cultures. We need to realise that in the ancient world people were trained to remember such oral narrative very accurately. These words were then written down by different people at different times. The first five books of the Bible include the narratives about creation, Noah and the flood, Abraham, Joseph and the other patriarchs. The rest of the Old Testament was written by different people, from scribes to prophets and historians. It is not in chronological order and some stories are told in several different books from different people's perspectives. Although it includes much history, it is not meant to be primarily a history book, but a book that demonstrates God's involvement with His chosen people Israel over many different periods of history. If you try to write a book that journals your family history over many different years, it would sound different from others' views of the same time period. This is the same if you look at Matthew, Mark, Luke and John, which are the first few books in the New Testament. They are based on eyewitness accounts of different people's times with Jesus. They are a great read, and they help us to know Jesus better.

In the early church the people had the Old Testament as their Bible. They read it, learnt it and quoted it. Jesus had quoted it a lot, too. Then the people who have been called the early church fathers decided, with much prayer, which of the letters and books to include in what is now known as the New Testament. Some of the books that were not included are found in a book called the Apocrypha. They are a great read, but we do not see them as the God-breathed living word of God.

There are now many different versions of the Bible. They are all translations from the original languages the Bible was written in. All of them say pretty much the same thing, but it is amazing how it sounds very different in each version.

So how do I read the Bible?
The first rule is that it is best not to start at the beginning like a normal book! Eventually, that is a great thing to do, but not until you understand some of the key principles. The best

place to start is the first few books of the New Testament: Matthew, Mark, Luke and John. These are called the 'Gospels' (meaning good news), as they tell us what Jesus did while He walked this earth. The different books all provide various (compatible) accounts of the events, and different angles on the same incidents involving Jesus. The guys tell us what Jesus was like, what kind of things He did and said. They are powerful, exciting books which help us understand more about Jesus, to whom we are giving our lives. His teachings are mind blowing and His actions were phenomenal. These books have to be read as soon as you can. Read them with a hunger to know Him!

The other good place to start is the Book of Psalms. These are poems, many of them written by King David, who had a fairly wild life, and they can be found in the middle of the Old Testament. They give us an insight into his relationship with God. My summary of the psalms would sound something like this: 'Oh God you are awesome, I'm constantly amazed at your goodness. I love to remember all the great things you have done. My life sucks at the moment God; I can't stop crying because it's so rough. However, I know you're with me and know me; you're my anchor and my rock. Thanks for being there for me. I love to praise you and sing to you all the time.'

You cannot summarise 150 chapters of poems adequately, but I just want you to get an idea of how real and refreshing they are! They are actually all different. Some are prayers of desperation and others are wonderful songs of praise. They can all be used to help us pray. Sometimes, as you open the Psalms, there is just one that expresses exactly how you feel, which can be so encouraging and helpful.

Bible study notes, useful for helping to explain small bits of the Bible at a time and how to apply it straight to your life, are available from Christian bookshops —or ask a friend.

Getting the Bible in your heart

The important thing is to understand that, even if you have read the Bible a hundred times and know everything in it, unless you allow God to let it soak into your heart, you are missing the point. Paul wrote, 'knowledge puffs up, but love edifies', so clearly the point of reading the Bible is certainly not to get a whole load of facts and information into our heads in order to feel really clever! The point is to hear what God is saying to us. As you read it, ask yourself, 'How does this change my life?' 'What does Jesus want to tell me here?' Then the best thing to do is to stop, pray, and wait for Him to touch your insides with His truth. Sometimes I only read one verse, and that can be enough to get me thinking and hearing God's thoughts! Another time I might end up reading a whole load. Sometimes I feel like it is directly speaking to me, and at other times I just find it helpful and interesting. I know that God always wants to tell me something, so I chill and wait and think! That can be called 'meditating'! To meditate does not mean that you sit with crossed legs and hum, and it is certainly not about emptying the mind, but rather, it involves thinking about and 'chewing over' each word in a sentence!

So get on with reading the Bible, and expect God to bring revelations to change your world!

Questions to think about

1. Do I understand that the Bible is relevant today?
2. Do I understand how to start reading it?
3. Are there any questions about it that are putting me off reading it, which I need to ask someone about?
4. Have I read one of the 'Gospel' books (Matthew, Mark, Luke or John)?

5

THE HOLY SPIRIT

The Holy Spirit is God! The Holy Spirit was given to those
of us who follow Jesus, to be with us and empower us on
this earth. He is a person of the Trinity, the awesome three
in one: the Father, Son and Holy Spirit. If you do not quite
understand how God can be three in one, then welcome to the
human race! There is no way in the world that we will ever
understand everything about God as He is infinitely greater
than we can imagine. We cannot understand everything
with our minds!

The big fact is that the Holy Spirit was there at the creation
of the world and is here now, so we can have a relationship
with Him. When the first church was started, the Holy Spirit
came to the people and impacted them amazingly, with His
reality, power and presence. (See Acts chapter 2.) The life
changing point of this chapter is that walking with the Holy
Spirit is awesome. We need to learn to walk with Him and
let Him work in us. If we do not do this, our entire life as a
follower of Jesus will probably become dry, dull and difficult
after a while. So let us find out about Him.

Who is the Holy Spirit?
The Holy Spirit is a person who is with us all the time. Isn't
that amazing? It has been said that, when we wake up in the

morning, it is only polite, therefore, to say 'Good morning, Holy Spirit'! He is with us to empower, equip, encourage and strengthen us.

It is up to us, though, to learn to allow Him to do that, by building our relationship with Him. When we understand that He is there to help us, it is easier to know what to do when we need strength or wisdom, for example. Jesus promised His disciples that He would never leave them:

> And I will pray the Father, and He will give you another Helper, that He may abide with you forever —the Spirit of truth, whom the world cannot receive, because it neither sees Him nor knows Him; but you know Him, for He dwells with you and will be in you. I will not leave you orphans; I will come to you.
>
> *John 14:16–18*

So, even if we feel alone, Jesus is telling us that we really are never alone! He is with us always, so we have to train our eyes (the eyes of our heart) to see – or be aware of – Him!

Jesus also spoke to His disciples just before He went to heaven:

> ...He commanded them...to wait for the Promise of the Father.... "...you shall receive power when the Holy Spirit has come upon you; and you shall be witnesses to Me in Jerusalem, and in all Judea and Samaria, and to the end of the earth."
>
> *See Acts 1:4, 8*

Here we see that the Holy Spirit brings us power. The power that Jesus speaks of will change us, and will give us stories to tell our friends, so that they will come to find Jesus too.

A few descriptions of the work of the Holy Spirit

The activity of the Holy Spirit is described in many ways in the Bible, and these descriptions help us understand more of who He is and what He does.

He is described as 'descending like a dove'; so He is gentle, harmless and pure. One of the results of the Holy Spirit moving on us is that we can feel freedom, and the 'dove' picture reminds us of this too. (See Matthew 3:16.) When the Holy Spirit came upon the disciples, they saw fire (Acts 2:3); and, like the action of fire, He refines and changes us with power and energy. Fire is a description also used in the Bible for passion, and the Holy Spirit brings passion and enthusiasm. He is described as helping us in many other ways that we shall look at in this chapter.

So how do I get filled with the Holy Spirit?

Once you realize how much we all need to be filled with the power of God, it is simply a case of asking! When you make the decision to become a Christian, the Holy Spirit wants to fill you, bring revelation of His love for you to your heart, and bring empowering into your life. Sometimes people forget to ask for this, or are never told that this IS the deal of being a follower of Jesus, and they wander around for years never having been filled with the Holy Spirit, feeling confused as to why they feel so dry. So, if you have not already done this, it is best to have a special moment when you and He get together, for you to ask for an empowerment! This is sometimes called being 'baptised in the Holy Spirit', and sometimes being 'filled with the Holy Spirit'.

When the Holy Spirit came to the disciples this is what happened:

When the Day of Pentecost had fully come, they were all with one accord in one place. And suddenly there came a sound from heaven, as of a rushing mighty wind, and it filled the whole house where they were sitting. Then there appeared to them divided tongues, as of fire, and one sat upon each of them. And they were all filled with the Holy

Spirit and began to speak with other tongues, as the Spirit gave them utterance.

Acts 2:1–4

Wow, does that sound awesome? Now it does not always feel just like that. Sometimes it does. A friend of mine, who was becoming interested in following Jesus, had started coming to church and had spent about five months asking God to reveal Himself to her. One night she rang me to ask if she had had an encounter with God. She said that she had awoken in the night to hear the sound of 'roaring wind'; she felt a buzzing all over her body, she felt an overwhelming sense of love, and knew that God could do anything. She said it was a totally overwhelming experience which she could not talk about for hours. I told her to read Acts 2, and she was amazed —she had no idea that this was what had happened to the people in the early church. Unsurprisingly, she gave her life to Jesus that week. Several others in church, who were in a similar stage of seeking God, wanted the same experience, but God gave them totally different ones. They are all now growing and flourishing in the house of God, with their kids. If you can, it is best to get a friend or someone in the church to pray for you, but if not, why not pray now? (Unless you are on a packed out train! I have had several 'Holy Spirit moments' on a train, and it is often a little amusing to my neighbours as they watch tears stream down my smiling face, with my eyes closed and earphones on!)

So what do you do?
• Understand that He wants to fill you and empower you.
• Ask Him to do that in a time when you are able to focus on Him.
• Wait for Him with a heart that is hungry to be filled with whatever He has for you.
• Do not be impatient…good things come to those who wait for Him! And wait with anticipation.
• Do not try a passive, half-hearted, non-believing wait! Press in to Him!

- Go with the flow!
- You may feel a great sense of peace and calm.
- Some people are overwhelmed with an understanding of His love.
- Some people know the power of God and feel 'blown away'!
- Some people do not feel anything, because they are too scared about what they will feel or will not feel! You may be all uptight, so your insides are all boxed up and hidden and you are using your mind! That does not work! God wants to impact your insides, so you need to come out from hiding and trust Him! You need to give Jesus your heart, and trust Him —that He knows what you need, what your fears are, and He wants to help you.

We are not all the same, so our initial experience of God may be different from someone else's experience, and that is great!

Doing that often
The thing is that Jesus wants us to have encounters with Him all the time like that. It becomes a life-long experience. We, as humans, seem to leak, and so need infilling all the time! We need to make time to wait on the Holy Spirit to work in us and bring His revelation and empowering. Without that we can become dry, boring, tired, disillusioned people. It becomes precious time with the Holy Spirit where we connect, and sense purpose and destiny!

So, then, how do I walk with the Holy Spirit?
Walking with the Holy Spirit is learning to be aware of His presence all the time. Even in the back of your mind, while you are working, it is awesome to be aware of Him, knowing that He wants to equip you there and then. The Holy Spirit can be whispering wisdom to you to help you at work, in relationships, or with your kids. He wants to develop in us a leaning in our heart to hear Him. It is a bit like when you first fall in love. Even when you are doing things totally unrelated,

there is a twinkle in your eye that maybe other people can see. You know in your insides that there is someone you love, who loves you, and that makes you smile!

Walking with Him includes obeying Him, and being sensitive to what hurts Him. When you fall in love, you develop an ability to be sensitive to that person and avoid habits that would irritate them, places they do not like, and certain words or actions that would hurt them. To walk with the Holy Spirit is really only possible if there is a desire to be sensitive to Him and sensitive to what hurts Him. Sin hurts Him, and obedience brings intimacy. To obey what is written in the Bible as the commands of God; to be aware of disobedience, and to repent when necessary —removes barriers to enable an ease and a flow!

The works of the Holy Spirit
When the disciples were empowered by the Holy Spirit, they immediately did some fairly great things. Peter stood up to preach, to explain what had just happened to the crowd that were looking on, and this is what happened:

> Then those who gladly received his word were baptized; and that day about three thousand souls were added to them. And they continued steadfastly in the apostles' doctrine and fellowship, in the breaking of bread, and in prayers. Then fear came upon every soul, and many wonders and signs were done through the apostles.
>
> *Acts 2:41–43*

So they could do signs and wonders. That means that the apostles were able to see people healed and set free; they could prophesy, and see miracles happen —in the name of Jesus. That means that we can, too!

Signs and wonders
The Holy Spirit wants to equip us to do the same works as Jesus did when He walked the earth. In the Gospel of John, Jesus says:

"Most assuredly, I say to you, he who believes in Me, the works that I do he will do also; and greater works than these he will do, because I go to My Father.

"And whatever you ask in My name, that I will do, that the Father may be glorified in the Son.

"If you ask anything in My name, I will do it."

John 14:12–14

So how do we get to do the works of Jesus?

We learn to step out in faith and try! Jesus said that He only did what He saw the Father doing, and you will notice that He did not heal everyone that He saw, and He did not do miracles everywhere. He did what the Father told Him! We are to learn to do what Jesus is telling us, and to pray for the sick, to prophesy over people —and see miracles happen. It is not stuff that only happens in church meetings; Jesus wants to see us doing His works everywhere! Miracles happen when people need something amazing to happen which could not take place without supernatural intervention. We love to pray at work for machines to be mended in the name of Jesus, for finances to be provided, for sicknesses to be gone, for keys to be found, for wisdom to be released, etc. People usually watch, and go: 'Wow! That's pretty cool!' They cannot deny that it is supernatural, and that the name of Jesus was phenomenally powerful.

Prophecy is a supernatural gift, where the person has a hunch or an impression that they tell another person. It is prophetic, because it is information that means a huge amount to the person receiving it, who recognises that they would not know it unless something supernatural had occurred. It is simplest for people to accept that it was a message from God, who knows the details of our lives and loves us! There are ways the Bible gives for testing to see whether a prophecy is genuine. The main purpose of prophecy is to build people up and encourage them, and not at all to judge or accuse them.

What about tongues?

Now this is the bit that freaks people out! I think it is the way that the media portray it as wacky, strange people losing all sense of normality and getting caught in a cult speaking in tongues. However, don't skip this bit! It is not that odd. No, OK it is quite odd, but it is great and awesome. Do not be put off by any preconceptions and wrong thinking.

'Tongues' is a way of our inside communicating to God. God is Spirit, and our spirit inside us often longs to connect to God, but our logical, small brain gets in the way. We want to pray something, but our head laughs and doubts. Speaking in tongues enables us to talk to Jesus at a deeper level. We do not know what we are saying, but that enables us to be praying in tongues, gently, under our breath, when we are thinking about something totally different. As we pray in tongues, it often helps us to connect and awaken ourselves to His presence. Sometimes, as we pray in tongues, we can receive His wisdom or guidance more quickly.

> For he who speaks in a tongue does not speak to men but to God, for no one understands him; however, in the Spirit he speaks mysteries.... He who speaks in a tongue edifies himself....
>
> *1 Corinthians 14:2, 4b*

So to speak in tongues edifies us —which means it builds us up, to be stronger and firmer.

How do I get the gift of tongues?

Firstly, ask; and believe that you can have the gift! Paul obviously thought that we could all have this gift because he says, 'I wish you all spoke with tongues' (1 Corinthians 14:5). He does not go on to say 'Too bad that only some of us can have it!' Secondly, make sure you have time to wait in His presence. Thirdly, be prepared to move your mouth! So many people think that God is going to make their mouth move as you burst into another language, and yet although sometimes this can happen, usually if you are sealing your mouth closed God is not likely to go against your will. Move your mouth by whispering your love to Jesus. Connect your heart, lose yourself in His presence, and be prepared to speak what you may feel is rubbish! 'Tongues' is often not a full on, foreign language. If it does not happen the first time, please do not feel like a failure but just keep pressing in without getting stressed and upset. Chill, worship and connect.

What other gifts of the Holy Spirit are there?
In 1 Corinthians 12, Paul talks about other gifts that we can have to help each other. There are all sorts of gifts, including words of knowledge or wisdom; healing, prophecy, discernment, etc. We can use all of them, but there will probably be one or two that God wants to especially release in your life! So start asking, and see what God gives you a passion for. Then use it so that it can grow and get stronger and more mature.

The Holy Spirit helps us in our walk with Jesus
He will guide me. (See Acts 8:29.)
He will give me peace that passes all understanding.
(See John 14:27.)
He will give me assurance of my salvation.
(See Romans 8:14–17.)
He will teach me. "But the helper, the Holy Spirit, whom the Father will send in My name, He will teach you all things...." (See John 14:26.)
He will comfort me. (See John 14:16.)
He will make me aware of my sin. (See John 16:8.)
He will help me to tell others about Jesus. (See Acts 1:8.)
He will give me gifts to be used to build the kingdom of God.
(See 1 Corinthians 12:4–11.)
He strengthens me. (See Ephesians 3:16.)
He pours out the love of God in our hearts.
(See Romans 5:5.)
He gives life. (See Luke 11:13.)

Questions to think about

1. Have I been filled with the Holy Spirit?
2. Have I begun to learn to wait on the Holy Spirit?
3. Have I used any gifts of the Holy Spirit, or watched anyone else use them?
4. Have I asked for His help and prayed for miracles?

6

BAPTISM A.S.A.P.

This chapter is all about being baptised in water. Being baptised is an awesome, significant experience that we are commanded to do by Jesus. In our culture, a whole lot of people seem to put off being baptised for ages after they have decided to follow Jesus, as if it is some optional extra. People seem to misunderstand how totally vital and significant baptism is.

In Acts, we read that there were three thousand people converted after Peter's preaching. It then says:

> Then those who gladly received his word were baptized; and that day about three thousand souls were added to them.
>
> *Acts 2:41*

This implies that they were not added to the number until they were baptised. Jesus commands baptism. He tells His disciples to,

> "Go therefore and make disciples of all the nations, baptizing them in the name of the Father and of the Son and of the Holy Spirit, teaching them to observe all things

that I have commanded you; and lo, I am with you always,
even to the end of the age...."

Matthew 28:19

So clearly, it is the thing to do as soon as you have 'become
a Christian', or decided to make Jesus the centre of your
life. It is not an optional extra for those people who do not
mind being in public. We recognise that, for a lot of people,
the thought of being in front of others, doing something so
personal and therefore vulnerable, seems to terrify them; but
we try to make it as comfortable as possible for people. We
do not want people to be robbed of the freedom that they
will know, by their fear of man.

Jesus Himself was baptised. Look what happened:

...it came to pass that Jesus also was baptized; and while
He prayed, the heaven was opened. And the Holy Spirit
descended in bodily form like a dove upon Him, and a voice
came from heaven which said, "You are My beloved Son;
in You I am well pleased."

Luke 3:21b–22.

The heavens opened over Jesus' life, for the Holy Spirit to
empower Him. An open heaven over our life means that
there is nothing stopping all that heaven wants to impart to
us being imparted! Yeehar! How beautiful is that!

What stops some people from being baptised?
The fear of man is that thing which keeps us from 'making
fools of ourselves' —that feeling, or terror, which many of us
feel, at the thought of what others may think of us. For many
people, this fear traps them into doing things that they do
not want to do, and not doing things they want to do. In the
Book of Proverbs in the Bible it says, 'The fear of man brings
a snare' (Proverbs 29:25). This fear can often keep people
away from the very thing that will set them free. If you have
a problem with the fear of man, the best way to see yourself

free from it is to pray, repent and then do something that kills it! Do something that makes it scream inside of you, 'Oh, how embarrassing' (as long as it is not rude or inappropriate!) —and you will sense a freedom come onto your life as you do it. Baptism is a great thing to do to break the power of such 'bondage' in your life. (Although that is not the main purpose, of course.)

What is baptism?

In our baptism services, the person who wants to get baptised is physically supported by two people, as they gently allow them to go backwards under the water —and then back up again. There is usually a great clap and cheer as all the people stand there, soaking wet and grinning. We are all so excited to see it, because we know that it is a significant point in someone's life, where they are really committing themselves to putting Jesus' teaching above their own reasoning. The Greek word 'baptise' means 'immerse', and the same word was used to speak of immersing a cloth in dye. That is why we believe that it is important to totally immerse the person in the water.

What does it symbolize?

It symbolizes the dying of our old self and the beginning of our new life with Jesus. The going under the water symbolizes the death to the old way of life, and the standing up again is the symbol of the new life. How cool is that? So we do not have to die like Jesus did for us, but we can remember that because He did, we can get baptised and have a brand new life! It symbolizes being washed by Jesus' blood. (See Revelation 1:5.)

Baptism is an outward experience to demonstrate what has gone on inside us.

There is an antitype which now saves us—baptism (not the removal of the filth of the flesh, but the answer of a good conscience toward God), through the resurrection of Jesus Christ, who has gone into heaven and is at the right hand of God, angels and authorities and powers having been made subject to Him.

1 Peter 3:21–22

What about christening or confirmation before I became a Christian?

If you were christened or baptised as a baby, that is a very different thing! The thing is that baptism needs to be on the back of your own personal decision, and not your parents' decision! So whatever has happened in the past is great, but really irrelevant, as it is now that you have met Jesus, and it is now that you need to demonstrate that relationship as a decision that you personally want to make.

The Bible seems to imply that baptism needs to be by full immersion, as the people in the New Testament were usually baptised in rivers. So in my view that is the best thing. Jesus was baptised in a river, but most of our rivers in the UK are a little chilly and polluted, so any pool of water does the job. It is important that it is not in a bath on your own, but a public experience, as being a Christian is being a part of a family who care, and who love you. It is also very powerful for you and others, as you tell people why you want to get baptised.

So get on with it, and get baptised!

Questions to think about

1. Do I understand what baptism is?
2. Do I understand the symbolism of it?
3. Have I got baptised? If not, have I asked when the next baptism is at church?

7

SORTING OUT YOUR
THOUGHT LIFE

This has to be one of the most important things that we learn as we follow Jesus. In our society, people do not seem to think it matters what you think, as long as it does not hurt anyone. However, in the Bible we can see that our thought life can build or destroy our lives. Jesus said, "...out of the abundance of the heart the mouth speaks" (Matthew 12:34a). This implies that we cannot keep our thoughts separate from our words and our world! In Romans 12:2, Paul tells us, 'And do not be conformed to this world, but be transformed by the renewing of your mind....'

Again in Proverbs 23:7 we read, 'For as he thinks in his heart, so is he.' This statement is amazing, as it implies that the essence of who we are is in our thought life. So we need to make sure that our thoughts are changing to become more like Jesus, too.

The power of our thoughts
The thing is if our minds are not renewed, then we can only change our actions in the short term. So, let us say that you have grown used to thinking that people are annoying, irritating and take up too much of your time. You have spent years thinking that, and agreeing with others who you hang out with, that that is true. Suddenly, you meet Jesus and

realize that He loves all people. You try to love people too, so you start to try to be nice to people, but inside you there is a tape going around your head saying: 'Yeah right, they'll only waste your time and ruin your life. Why am I bothering?' After years of listening to lies about people, it is time to start to renew your mind with truth!

Let us take another example. Suppose that you were brought up as someone who had to earn your love by being good, successful or funny. Then you meet Jesus. Usually that thought pattern does not change overnight. You begin to love being with Jesus, but deep down you really think that He only loves you when you are good, successful or funny. Your head knows the truth that He loves you all the time, and that you cannot earn His love because it is a gift that He freely gives to you, but you cannot quite stop the niggling feeling that that is not true! Something needs to be done. It is your mind that needs to be renewed.

So how do we renew our minds?
Once you realize that to renew your mind starts off with a revelation, and then a decision, you are off to a great start! It is good to know that changes to your world will happen with some changes happening to your mind. It is an awesome adventure finding out what rubbish is stored in the lining of our minds and knowing that we have been given the power to get rid of it and replace it with truth. It is life changing stuff. Once you realize that there are some rubbish thoughts dominating your subconscious, you can take them to Jesus. For example, if I had a problem with knowing that Jesus loved me just as I was, then I would start by telling Him so. I would pour out my heart to Him and let Him heal me and comfort me. Then I would ask Him to show me what actual sentences are affecting my mind. I usually find that there are sentences which prevent the truth from taking hold —words which have been spoken in my subconscious for so many years that they have become like a 'mind tape'. So I ask Him to show me what those are, and I ask Him to break the power of those words over my life and replace them with truth. So

I listen to Him, and what He really thinks about me, and I let that soak into my heart. Then I will learn a verse that tells me that Jesus loves me, and I will learn to say that verse whenever the old negative thoughts come back. It is just replacing the bad with the good. Sometimes the process is quick because there has been a Holy Spirit given revelation, and at other times it seems to be a battle to learn to listen to truth. But truth brings life and freedom, so it is worth fighting for. The way to success in our thought life is, 'bringing every thought into captivity to the obedience of Christ.' (See 2 Corinthians 10:5.)

So how do we know what thoughts need renewing?
This process of renewing our mind is a lifelong journey that we are all on, as we realize more and more what Jesus taught and what His truth is. Any thoughts that we recognise or catch that do not seem to line up with what the Bible says need to be changed. It can be quite amazing to see how much of our culture has become 'truth' to us. It can be hard to distinguish what we actually do believe from what our culture has told us we believe. So much seems to seep into our subconscious by 'mistake'. For example, we are aware that most of our ideas of how to look good come directly from what the media tell us. What we think is beautiful is different from what other cultures think is beautiful. We know that fact, but it can be so difficult to tell our subconscious that it's OK to be totally different. Our minds need renewing! Remember that the enemy of our souls wants us to believe him. He wants to destroy us, and one of his main tactics is to rob us from our inheritance of real freedom and joy by keeping our minds locked in lies. Jesus teaches us that the truth sets us free, so dwell on His truth, and allow Him to bring revelations to your mind and soul. We need to be on a mission to banish lies from our minds!

What do we feed our minds?
The fact is that we have an enormous amount of choice of what to feed our minds. We can choose which books to

read, which films to watch, what television programmes to see, and who to spend our time with. Paul wrote to the church to say:

> Finally, brethren, whatever things are true, whatever things are noble, whatever things are just, whatever things are pure, whatever things are lovely, whatever things are of good report, if there is any virtue and if there is anything praiseworthy —meditate on these things.
>
> *Philippians 4:8*

That is quite a clear instruction, that tells us to fill our minds and feed our minds with helpful and edifying thoughts. To fill our heads with dark, nasty, evil, rude or impure thoughts, will cause our mind to be more familiar with dark, nasty, evil and impure things, rather than the things of God. Come on people —it is so obvious! People struggle with fear, and yet they force themselves to watch horror movies, thinking that will help them! Whatever you feed your mind on will have influence over your thoughts, reactions, actions, and beliefs. Do not expect to spend five minutes with Jesus every day and the other sixteen waking hours being brainwashed by what society says is normal, and then see your life changed. A great proportion of our current society thinks that it is normal to spend hours of our leisure time dwelling on violence, crime, murder, porn, witchcraft stories, tales full of hatred and lust. They do not realize how corrupt this is.

Jesus said, "The lamp of the body is the eye...." (See Luke 11:34.) You might think of your mind as being like a canvas. Guard your eyes, so that your soul can be a canvas that the Holy Spirit can paint on. He can paint dreams, visions, revelations, truth and creative thoughts on a mind that dwells on Him.

How do I know what to read, watch and listen to?
We are all made differently, and we all need to learn how much we are influenced by what medium. For example, my husband is influenced much less than me by what he

watches, so he can be a little less cautious in that area. I find it more difficult to get images erased from my head that I have seen on a screen. Therefore I am strict about what I watch, as I want my mind to be a pure and fertile ground for Jesus to speak to me. A mind that is full of dodgy, horrific images could well struggle to have revelations of beauty and purity. However, there is not a point where you can say that you are so mature you are not affected by images which are not helpful. That would be denying the truth of what the Bible says, and agreeing instead with those in our society who say we are not affected by what we see. But many psychologists do now agree that maybe the rise in violent films and computer games could be affecting behaviour patterns in our culture. The key for us who love Jesus is to learn to nurture our conscience, which should be open to the prompting of the Holy Spirit whispering what is right and wrong. We have usually learned to put our fingers in our ears and not listen to Him, and it is simply a case of learning once again to listen. If you want to know what is right and wrong, He will surely show you!

The best thing to feed your mind on
That has to be obvious. The Bible is the word of God, and the more we fill our minds and allow our souls to feed on that, the more life we will know. Jesus says, "I have come that they may have life, and that they may have it more abundantly" (John 10:10b).

Never let your thoughts start to breed self pity, because you have to give up dwelling on bad stuff. If you think that you are doing God a favour, you have really missed the point. He wants to breathe His life and freedom into you. If you think that that is boring, then you have forgotten that we are talking about the God who created surfing, sex, mountains, and slugs —the whole universe, in fact! Giving up dwelling on bad stuff should be the natural reaction to meeting Jesus, but sometimes people get confused, so this chapter is trying to help you avoid wasting months or years. Dwell on Him, let Him paint on the canvas of your soul, feed on His word, and you will find that life really does get more abundant in a huge number of often unexpected ways.

Questions to think about

1. Do I recognise any 'mind tapes' which are lies that are stopping me believing the truth that Jesus is saying?
2. Do I understand how to renew my mind?
3. Do I understand what to feed my mind on?

8

WHAT ABOUT MONEY?

You may wonder why this chapter is included in the top ten subjects to help to get Jesus as the centre of your life. It is important to realise that Jesus gave us some important teaching about money, and the Bible recognises that it is a subject that causes some emotional reactions. People can often struggle to have enough money, and so develop a love-hate relationship with it, which can mean that jealousy and bitterness lie in the fibre of their being. Other people have always had plenty, yet still want more in order to appease their insatiable appetite for more material things, status and pleasure. Money can become addictive. Yet money can be a huge blessing. So how would Jesus want us to understand and manage money?

Jesus was not poor
The first place to start is the major preconception that most people have about Jesus and money. Most people seem to believe that Jesus was born poor, lived a poor and meagre life, and died poor. Some Christmas carols that we sing seem to continually imply that Jesus was poor. However, we read that when He was a child He was given gifts of gold, frankincense and myrrh.

"Where is He who has been born King of the Jews? For we have seen His star in the East and have come to worship Him...."

And when they had come into the house, they saw the young Child with Mary His mother, and fell down and worshipped Him. And when they had opened their treasures, they presented gifts to Him: gold, frankincense, and myrrh.

Matthew 2:2 and 11

In that period of history it would have been incredibly rude to give a tiny amount of these precious substances to a king, so we know that Jesus was given a large amount. We know, too, that whilst Jesus travelled there was a need for a treasurer to help look after finances. Judas was entrusted with custody of the money.

But one of His disciples, Judas Iscariot, Simon's son, who would betray Him, said, "Why was this fragrant oil not sold for three hundred denarii and given to the poor?"

This he said, not that he cared for the poor, but because he was a thief, and had the money box; and he used to take what was put in it.

John 12:4–6

So cash was evidently needed and available.

What did He teach about money?

Paul taught, 'For the love of money is a root of all kinds of evil, for which some have strayed from the faith in their greediness, and pierced themselves through with many sorrows' (1Timothy 6:10). Sadly, many Christians have forgotten the beginning of that sentence, and have misinterpreted it, thinking that having any money is evil. But Paul did not say that; rather, he pointed to the *love* of money being a root of all kinds of evil. Jesus taught that we are not to worry about money and provision for the things we need. He said,

"Therefore do not worry, saying, 'What shall we eat?' or 'What shall we drink?' or 'What shall we wear?' For after all these things the Gentiles seek. For your heavenly Father knows that you need all these things. But seek first the kingdom of God and His righteousness, and all these things shall be added to you. Therefore do not worry about tomorrow...."

Matthew: 6:31ff.

He also shows us that hoarding earthly possessions and money is a bad and empty focus for our lives that will not make us happy.

"Do not lay up for yourselves treasures on earth, where moth and rust destroy and where thieves break in and steal; but lay up for yourselves treasures in heaven, where neither moth nor rust destroys and where thieves do not break in and steal. For where your treasure is, there your heart will be also."

Matthew 6:19–21

Many in our society seem to believe that if only they had that one last thing they would be happy. I see it with my kids all the time. 'Oh please, Mummy, I won't want anything else, I promise. If I can get those sweets, I'll never want any more. Those ones are all I want.' My children really do mean it for that hour —until the next thing catches their eye. Jesus teaches us to go against the flow of our culture and be more concerned with storing spiritual treasure in heaven, by obeying Him and loving others, than by collecting material goods! But this does not mean that we cannot enjoy earthly possessions.

Jesus as the centre

The main key to all this talk about money is to be found in those final verses: 'Where your treasure is, there your heart will be' and 'seek first the kingdom of God and His righteousness, and all these things shall be added to you.'

Some people are almost scared about money because they feel that they may grow to like it too much. They decide to live a meagre life to avoid the temptation of riches. This is not the way forward. Jesus wants us to have all that we need, and more. The key to not letting money 'have you' is to make sure that you seek Jesus and His righteousness *first*, and seek treasure in heaven *first*. That is true, whether you do not have enough money at the moment or you have lots!

All we have we have given to Jesus

The thing is that when we decided to give our lives to Jesus it meant that we gave Him the key to our bank and wallet. It all became His. We are simply the stewards of His money. That is great news, because if we have needs and we have put Him first, then it is not really our problem. It is God's money, and He will help us. The other good news is that He helps us to know what it is right to do with the money that is in our accounts. He wants to bless us and prosper us with all that we need for abundant life. (See John 10:10.) He wants to bless us so that we can be a blessing to all those around us. In the story of the Good Samaritan there is a very important point which you may not have noticed. The story goes that there was a man who was robbed and beaten up. Several men walked past and did not care for this poor man. Eventually a Samaritan guy walks up to him, tends him, puts him on a donkey and takes him to a hotel. There he pays for the injured man's entire stay until he has recovered. One of the morals of the tale is that we are to do the same. How is that possible if we are totally poor? I want to be financially blessed so that I can pay for church buildings that speak of God's glory and magnitude, drug addicts to be rehabilitated, banquets for homeless people, parties for the lonely, food for the hungry.... Do you?

Generosity: the hallmark of a disciple of Jesus

Jesus also teaches us about abundance. He teaches this by His actions as well as His words. He created abundantly and He loved abundance. When His mother asked Him to help at the wedding of a friend, He could have turned just enough water into wine, and everybody would have been blessed and happy. If we read the story carefully we notice that He turned so much water into wine that they had buckets and buckets left over! Similarly, both times He fed the crowds with bread and fish they had a lot left afterwards.

> So they all ate and were filled, and they took up twelve baskets full of the fragments that remained.
>
> *Matthew 14:20*

> So they all ate and were filled, and they took up seven large baskets full of the fragments that were left.
>
> *Matthew 15:37*

I am noticing a pattern. Jesus was incredibly generous. He clearly did not worry about having enough. He also encourages us to give abundantly. He shows us that if someone wants to try to get as much from us as possible, we should surprise them with our generous attitude.

> "If anyone wants to sue you and take away your tunic, let him have your cloak also. And whoever compels you to go one mile, go with him two. Give to him who asks you, and from him who wants to borrow from you do not turn away."
>
> *Matthew 5:40*

Looking after the poor

There is a lot of teaching about being generous in the Old Testament as well. There are some scary words about how God views those people who hoard their belongings and ignore the poor. Most of the prophetic books talk about the need to look after the poor, the widows and the needy. The book of Isaiah makes some great promises for those of us who care for them. Isaiah is prophesying that God wants us to live as His followers, and not just talk about it and be religious. God hates the hypocrisy of empty religious talk and outwardly religious acts that lack care for those in need.

> "Is this not the fast that I have chosen:
> To loose the bonds of wickedness,
> To undo the heavy burdens,
> To let the oppressed go free,
> And that you break every yoke?
> Is it not to share your bread with the hungry,
> And that you bring to your house
> the poor who are cast out;
> When you see the naked, that you cover him,
> And not hide yourself from your own flesh?
> Then your light shall break forth like the morning.
> Your healing shall spring forth speedily,
> And your righteousness shall go before you;
> The glory of the LORD shall be your rear guard.
> Then you shall call, and the LORD will answer;
> You shall cry, and He will say, 'Here I am.'"
>
> *Isaiah 58:6–9*

More promises follow for those who help the poor. Read Isaiah 58 yourself. It is no use saying we want to be like Him if we are unprepared to love sacrificially. He wants us to love the unlovable, give to the needy, and care for those who are poor materially or spiritually.

Generosity in accordance with what you have
In following Jesus and learning to give, it is all about equal sacrifice, not equal giving. We do not all have the same amount of income. We are in different seasons and times in our lives, and we need to be generous in accordance with what God has given us. The story of the 'widow's two mites' teaches us that it is not the absolute amount of money that matters. She gave her few pennies, while the Pharisees gave lots of money; Jesus told them well and truly what He thought. He said:

"...Truly I say to you that this poor widow has put in more than all; for all these out of their abundance have put in offerings for God, but she out of her poverty put in all the livelihood that she had."

Luke 21:3f.

God sees our heart and knows how much we are putting Him first, and how much we are kidding ourselves. He wants to bring us to a place of freedom by putting Him first in everything. Then we can know life in all its fullness.

What is tithing and giving?

Tithing is giving 10% of our gross income to God. This helps us remember to put Jesus, His kingdom and His righteousness first. Remember Matthew 3:21ff, which we looked at earlier. As we seek first the kingdom of God and His righteousness, all that we need and more will be provided. The tithe is meant to be given to the church because God is very protective about His church. It is His bride, and He wants to ensure that it can be a powerful resource to bless the nations. People often have some funny thoughts about this and misunderstand the whole thing through hurt and confusion. The principle is that when we seek Jesus first 'all these things will be added to you'. I say 'gross income', because that is putting Jesus before the tax man! I believe that if you want all that Jesus has for you, it is actually not an optional extra. For some of us it causes conflict with our logic as we can mathematically work out how much more we would have a month if we did not tithe, and it can be just what we need. This can be a great opportunity to put God's ways first and our logical reasoning in its proper place.

The Israelites were told to give Him their firstfruits. We are to seek His kingdom first and trust He will give us all we need. He gives to us in ways that are outside our understanding.

Sowing and reaping

The principle of sowing and reaping is a natural law that God has put into this universe. A farmer sows seed in order to reap a harvest. The principle of sowing and reaping applies to all areas of our lives. God teaches us to sow generously so that we can reap a harvest. It is obvious as we look at areas like our friendships. As we sow into our friendships by spending time, remembering birthdays and hosting parties, we reap a harvest of birthday cards, invitations to parties and friendships. It is just natural! Regarding our finances, the Bible teaches us that we are to give generously, and He will look after us. We are to put His agenda first. As we give generously, God will, in time, ensure that we reap a harvest of provision and resources to bless others and to be blessed ourselves.

God's provision for us

God promises that He will look after us, providing all that we need. This can happen in a number of ways. I am sitting in my house now, aware of the miracle that it is. We sold our house some years ago, to release money to help with the start of the church that we lead. We sold it when the property market was starting to boom. We knew it was the right thing to do, despite people being concerned that it was not sensible in the circumstances. We sold the house and told all our friends and family that we were not living in the world's economy, but in God's economy, so it would be fine! We told the removal company that was coming to move all our belongings that we did not know what the address of the new house was yet, as we were waiting for a miracle to happen. We really did believe that God was going to drop a huge and beautiful house into our possession the day we moved out. On the week that we had to move, we realized that we may have to be a little more patient, and we arranged for all our possessions to go into storage. A member of the church rented us a tiny cottage for three weeks. Eight months later, with all our things still in storage, having slept on the floor of the lounge on mattresses, with two little children who wanted to know when we were going home, we were still determined to believe God's word above our experience. It says very clearly in Mark 10:29f.,

> "Assuredly, I say to you, there is no one who has left house or brothers or sisters or father or mother or wife or children or lands, for My sake and the gospel's, who shall not receive a hundredfold now in this time – houses and brothers and sisters and mothers and children and lands, with persecutions – and in the age to come, eternal life."

We never stopped praying for a miracle. Occasionally we got fed up, but mostly we visualized our new home and prayed for it room by room. Almost four years of renting later, we were asked to leave our rented house as the landlord was coming 'home'. We knew this was God's timing to release to us our miracle home. Eight weeks later we walked into the home that we had dreamt of, in the road that we had asked for, with a garden that the kids had prayed for! The money that we needed came from lots of different sources, and we did not ask, tell or in any way advertise our need. It was God's timing, and the home was released.

In the four years of our waiting for it, God had done lots of work in our life, including developing patience and a long term fight in our hearts for His word to prevail over people's own 'wisdom'. What a great journey!

All around our house we can see story after story of God's provision through amazing bargains, (which are almost always answers to prayer), the generosity of people and supernatural provision.

God is not limited to our own ideas about how He can provide for us. Do not imagine that there is a 'ceiling' on His power and provision for our lives!

Budgeting

This seems such an obvious thing to say, but it is difficult to see how much we are giving and needing unless we do a sensible budget. Without a budget the whole thing is guesswork and that is generally not a responsible way to deal with money. If you do not have a budget, try to write down all the regular outgoings and income, and then, if there is a shortfall, you know what you are praying for. Ask someone for help if you do not know where to start.

Let us be people who know God's miraculous provision, give generously, seek God's agenda first, and live lives where people want to know our source!

Questions to think about

1. Is money something that you know you have a hang up about?
2. Do you understand generosity and tithing?
3. Do you understand the principle of sowing and reaping?
4. Are you prepared to continue to have your mind renewed about money?

9

YOU CAN MAKE A DIFFERENCE

You were created at a specific time for a specific purpose!
God planned for you to live an extraordinary life serving His
purposes. He never planned for any of us to be ordinary. He
has given you dreams, gifts and longings that He has given no
one else. You are unique; there is no one else like you. God
does not make mistakes, and He designed you to have a life
full of His plans and purposes. He has things for you to do;
He promises to equip you with everything you need, and He
longs for you to know the freedom and excitement of living as
He planned for you —to live, knowing life in all its fullness.

For I know the thoughts that I think toward you, says the
LORD, thoughts of peace and not of evil, to give you a future
and a hope. Then you will call upon Me and go and pray
to Me, and I will listen to you. And you will seek Me and
find Me, when you search for Me with all your heart.

Jeremiah 29:11–13

...His divine power has given to us all things that pertain
to life and godliness....

See 2 Peter 1:2

Life is not meant to be an endless round of earning money, maintaining relationships, trying to achieve moving goals, sleeping and eating! Many people have tasted moments of pleasure when they did something that was significant, and said to themselves, 'Now I know why I'm alive.' God wants us to know that every day! He wants us to know in the depths of our beings that we have a destiny that is just for us. There is no one like you anywhere in the world, and there is no one that is called to do exactly what you are. Anyone excited out there?

Queen Esther had an exciting life when she was picked to be the queen and found herself in a position where she could save a whole nation. She chose to risk her life to obey God because she understood that she was born for exactly that moment in history. 'Yet who knows whether you have come to the kingdom for such a time as this?' (Esther 4:14.) She obeyed God, stuck her neck out by talking to the king and in effect 'telling on' an important guy in the palace, and she saved the Jews from death. God has a role for each of us —maybe significantly less dangerous than that, but maybe not!

How do I find out what my destiny is?
To know what your destiny is, you need to plug into the source of life. God wants to reveal His plans to us; often it is a great dream, and He will reveal the specifics when it becomes necessary. The thing to do is to allow God to paint a picture on the walls of your heart. As you worship Him and spend time with Him, allow yourself to dream dreams and see what is in your heart. What stirs you up inside? What excites you? The passion that you feel is not an accident but probably a gifting that He has placed in you. All the dreams, passions, gifts and desires that you have are there for the ultimate purpose of seeing God's kingdom extended here on earth. It is not all about me or you; it is all about Him, and His ways and His plans. As we give our ways up to Him, He breathes life and passion into our souls.

"But seek first the kingdom of God and His righteousness, and all these things shall be added to you."

Matthew 6:33

Serve Jesus and His purposes and He will release your dreams and gifts! If He is not first though, it all becomes a little dry and lifeless, because ultimately it is all selfish!

What is my gift?
Your gift does not have to be one of the gifts listed in the Bible. Those gifts are essential tools for building God's house, but there are plenty more. But here are some:

And God has appointed these in the church: first apostles, second prophets, third teachers, after that miracles, then gifts of healings, helps, administrations, varieties of tongues.

1 Corinthians 12:28

You feel a 'Yeah!' after some of those descriptions, and know that is you! Or you may feel a decided 'Uh?' and have no idea what you are called to do. The thing is that there is no mention of some other gifts that are totally vital in building the house of God. These include: toilet cleaning, security, painting, business skills, cooking, writing, singing, television production and other media, kids' entertaining, carpentry, architecture, etc. All of these gifts, and all the many that there is no space to list, are given to different people to use as their gifts. These are as vital to build the house of God. They need to be seen as tools that God has given us to build His house and His kingdom. They were not given to us to build our kingdom and make our lives comfortable, but to see His purposes achieved. So go and be a plumber, knowing that it is God who has called you, God who equips you, and God who wants you to be a successful and anointed plumber! There are people you are going to meet who are going to be blown away by your attitude, skills and excellence, and they will want to know your God. You are a minister of the gospel!

Is success a godly desire?

If you worry that it is wrong to believe that we are meant to be successful in what we do, I would like to ask you a question: Do you think that it is your aim in life to fail in your work; fail in your relationships and fail in your purposes? Exactly! There is no one who wants to fail, and we have a God who wants to equip us and empower us to succeed. When we do mess up, we know that it has happened to teach us something we never would have found out otherwise —which enables us to be more successful.

If we believe that God has gifted us, we know that others will confirm it in our lives. People will see it and desire to see the gift blossom and grow. If you would like others to do that to you, do you know where to start? Start by encouraging others and praying that their gifts blossom. Sometimes we have to be persistent in seeing what we believe in our hearts can happen here on earth. This enables us to develop a fighting spirit, a stronger sense of calling, and a faith that overcomes.

God has called us. God has gifted us. We are all called to be life changers. We are all called to build His house and see His purposes achieved. We all have a job to do and a unique role to play!

Serving others changes lives

Jesus has a lot to say about serving. The main thrust of serving is to live life wanting to love others, rather than living purely to make (or keep) ourselves happy.

Let nothing be done through selfish ambition or conceit, but in lowliness of mind let each esteem others better than himself. Let each of you look out not only for his own interests, but also for the interests of others.

Philippians 2:3–4

It is life changing stuff as we learn to trust that, as we look to serve others and, therefore, Jesus, He will look after us. It is a change from the 'if you don't look after yourself then no one else will' mentality. Jesus teaches us that it is no longer all about us as 'No 1'. That does not mean that we become doormats who are meagre, mild, empty beings who have no life unless others are blessed and we are trodden on. It means that we put Jesus first, and, as we do that, our lives take on His priorities —and that is where we find freedom and life.

Going against the consumer mentality

Serving others is not something that our society recognises as 'normal'. We live in a consumerist society, where we assume that we have a right to get what we feel we deserve. We have often got hold of the idea that we should be looked after by someone somewhere, and ultimately that very few things are our own responsibility. All the bad stuff that has happened to us is someone's fault. Now although sometimes it is not our own fault, as a lot of stuff can go wrong because of evil and other people's bad choices, often the rubbish we face is our own fault, and we are actually running away from any responsibility for making our own choices; not always, but sometimes. In our society at the moment, it seems to be quite acceptable to take anyone to court to sue them over something that seems to be an innocent mistake. People have become quite unreasonable about their 'rights'. Similarly, many people have lost the art of serving each other without return. Many of our friends who are not following Jesus seem to be very concerned about 'paying us back' if we have done them a favour. We can rarely manage to explain that we wanted to bless them for no ulterior purpose! We have to make an active decision to go against society's obsession with consumerism, and embrace serving as an exciting lifestyle.

In our communities: one life at a time!

God has put each of us in a certain place to live and work, and His plan is that we are able to show other people the good news of Jesus. We do not force people to listen to us as we talk to them about deep theology. Stuffing the good news of Jesus down people only causes them to be sick! We need to naturally talk about what God is doing in our life, but with an awareness that it is always best to say a bit and then wait for them to ask questions. When people ask us questions about Jesus, they want to know the answer. Jesus changes lives, doesn't He?

When He reveals His love, mercy and power to us, we do not stay the same and carry on with our day to day lives exactly as we had done. Suddenly, the whole purpose of our lives becomes clearer and clearer, and as we grow in our relationship with Jesus, our pains, hurts and confusions become less painful and confusing. Being with Jesus heals! He is the King of kings, the Creator, and the lover of your soul, and in His presence there will be found joy, healing, clarity and peace, among many other things. It is only natural that we will want our friends, neighbours and relations to know about Jesus.

One of the things that will change in our lives as Jesus impacts us is our attitude to other people. We want to be like Jesus, and we will therefore want to serve them and go out of our way to love them, even when they annoy us. We do not always feel like it, but we know that Jesus loves them, and who are we to withhold the love of God from them? As His kids, we represent Jesus on this planet, and His main characteristic is love. Therefore we need to love and love until it hurts. People who do not know Jesus can often be the most loving people, so it is not that we have to be more competitively loving than them, but we need to know that people listen to our actions more than our words. That is why in the Bible it says, 'Thus also faith by itself, if it does not have works, is dead' (James 2:17). Without love we are really rather opinionated, unpleasant people, even if we have the answer for the questions of life. Paul wrote, 'Though I speak with the tongues of men and of angels, but have not love, I have become sounding brass or a clanging cymbal' (1 Corinthians 13:1).

Serving our communities and friends by practically loving them is an opportunity to show them Jesus' love. We can have loads of fun by making cakes, offering lifts, listening to the lonely, speaking to the people who are left out, and actively listening to the Holy Spirit for ideas of how to help specific people at specific times. We can change a nation one person at a time.

Building God's house together

Our primary purpose in this earth is to build God's house, not our own —to do His will; to speak His words; to love the people He created; to see His kingdom established in this earth, as it is in heaven. Therefore church is a place where we are called to serve, build, work, love, cherish, protect, and nurture before our own house!

Yet people do seem to have a hard time understanding the house of God from a kingdom of God perspective. The crowds turn up at church excited about what God is going to do for them in the service, and that is a great thing —expectation is really important when we come to meet with God corporately. However, the thing is that we need to be aware that often the consumer mentality can kick in, which is a complete misunderstanding of church. People find themselves whining about the coffee being a little strong, or the music a little loud, or the message not quite as passionate as the week before. There seems to be a total misunderstanding of the role of those of us who are following Jesus. We are called to be builders of God's house and bringers of God's presence. I do not mean that we are all meant to become qualified builders, and literally build a new modern building. The church is described as God's house because it is a place where a bunch of His people seek Him and worship Him.

Our bodies are also described as God's temple, because we have given our lives to Jesus and have the Holy Spirit living in us. Paul teaches us that we therefore need to look after our bodies because they are important vessels.

To have an understanding of how we are all called to be builders in the house of God will cause churches to become awesome places that give glory to Him, where people are drawn in by the sense of purpose and the powerful presence of God. It is not a passive role but an active one. As a rule, builders usually get hot, sweaty and tired as they work hard to build a house. They know that sitting around all day looking at the house will not help it to be built! It is the same with church: we can all sit around and discuss the weaknesses and irritations that are there, but that does not build a stronger church. The way to build a strong church is for people to understand that they all have a role to play in building it, and that we are all going to get tired and sweaty at times, but we can be pleased as we look with satisfaction at a place that God is moving in, and where His kingdom is being established. The task of building the house of God is never finished —not until everyone knows Jesus. Therefore there is no time to sit back on our laurels, feeling chuffed with what we have done —although we should have time to enjoy all that we have done together, and feel a huge sense of thankfulness. It is this that very often builds the momentum and passion to see more of the same and better happen. We are a people who are determined to put God's house above our own, and serve in any way we can to see the job being done.

We often use the analogy of church being like a party. If it is Christmas and we are all there together, it really is not going to happen if only a few people bring presents for a few people. If everybody comes prepared to give, then it becomes an amazing party where everybody receives.

Finding your place to serve

It is really great to find the place where you fit in to serve in the house of God. In our church we try and encourage people to get stuck into serving in an area where they think or know that they are gifted. It is good for people to grow, blossom and be successful in that area. It is a privilege to help people spot what that gifting area could be, and see them released into it so that they can begin to fly. We need to see people moving in what God calls them to do, as we are all given specific gifts to use to see His house built.

We also encourage people to serve in a practical area where they feel it is a bit out of their comfort zone. Be careful when it all feels too comfortable. If we are always comfortable then there is probably little growing going on. Being stretched helps us all to allow God to continue to refine us and show us our attitudes. It is funny to watch those of us who are not used to practical serving, trying to kill the mind attitude that whispers, 'Isn't this a little bit below me?' We love to put ourselves into situations that allow God to show us where we are getting stuck in a rut with our serving. Having said that, it is not a great thing to see a preacher putting the chairs out just before he or she preaches —not if you value that word from God that is burning in his or her heart. If you want to receive revelation from God, you do need to treasure it in that preacher's heart, and bombarding them with practical problems can cause it to become less fresh.

It is all in the attitude

Having said that serving is really important, it is vital to say that serving with the right attitude is what counts. Have you ever been given presents by people who begrudgingly gave them? I bet you would rather have not had the present. When people serve with bad attitudes, it is usually much worse than if there were only a few people with cheerful attitudes. Clearly, many of us struggle with getting up early to put the chairs out, and do not always feel excited about going on the streets to feed the homeless after a long day at work, but when we do it knowing that it is worship to the heart of Jesus, that should change something! If we realize that our actions can bring pleasure to Him, it becomes a wonderful thing. It is a bit like being able to buy your special person something they really want; it brings the same kind of smile to my face. Remember, as well, that love is a decision, not a feeling; although the feeling often follows when actions kick in. We are not serving to earn our salvation, because that is a free gift. We are serving in the way that we know we are called to, because we want to worship Him.

God loves a cheerful giver, so choose to serve with joy, knowing that it is worship to our Father in heaven.

Excited to make a difference

So let us become an army of cheerful servants who depend on God for strength, knowing that it is our actions as well as our words that bring Jesus praise —a people who know that we are called to make a difference to the world around us and are not put off by the immensity of the task, but faithful to do what God has called us to do.

Let us be people who are prepared to see one life change at a time, but who impact hundreds —as an army of God's empowered servants, full of His Holy Spirit, unreligious, fun loving people; we can see phenomenal things happen which generations to come can talk about!

Questions to think about

1. Do I understand that I have a specific purpose, destiny, and job to do?
2. Have I made a decision to 'go for it' and make a difference to the people that God has put around me?
3. Do I naturally have a consumer mentality?
4. Do I have an attitude that is building or destroying God's house?

10

BEING LIKE JESUS

In this last chapter I want to briefly give you a few little thoughts that I believe could really help you as you become determined to grab a hold of all that God has for you. The thing that devastates me more than most things is when people seem to have a revelation of Jesus, but then lose the plot as they miss some fundamental truths that stop them knowing all the awesome things that Jesus has for them. If you do not know a freedom, joy, peace and a sense of being alive, despite your circumstances, then keep pressing in and asking God to reveal any things that are stopping you know it. He died that you would know life in this way, but there are some things that can hinder you knowing them. Come on! I ask you to have a determination to grow, blossom and keep seeking God's face, until more 'pennies drop' and revelations sink into the depths of your heart and change your life. Do not wait for it to happen to you; run after Him. "But seek first the kingdom of God and His righteousness, and all these things shall be added to you" (Matthew 6:33).

Do not settle for second best; do not settle for the 'at least I'm saved'. Let God burn a passion in your heart and change your life. Have an adventure! Life is not a dress rehearsal; you only have one opportunity. Go for it!

> Therefore we also, since we are surrounded by so great a cloud of witnesses, let us lay aside every weight, and the sin which so easily ensnares us, and let us run with endurance the race that is set before us, looking unto Jesus, the author and finisher of our faith....
>
> *Hebrews 12:1f.*

It does not talk about having a picnic but about running a race! We do not have to become all weird and intense about this. We will accomplish more in this life as we let God impact our hearts with His passion and joy; we will naturally be people that others want to be around.

Being like Jesus
We read in the New Testament that people wanted to be around Jesus (apart from some of the religious people), because He was fun, fascinating, holy, wise and wonderful. He was not a meek, pathetic, weak guy, but a man full of power, strength and goodness. Crowds followed Him around. We should want to be like Him, and becoming like Him is the process of giving our lives to Him. God says, 'Be holy, for I am holy' (1 Peter 1:16); and He planned for us to be transformed into His image. In the same way, as we spend time with friends, and catch some of their catchphrases, so also do we catch some of God's priorities as we spend time with His people, read His book and spend time with Him. Jesus wants to impact every area of our lives and bring them into line with His original plans for us. He wants us to become holy as He is holy. There is real freedom where there is holiness. He wants us to fight against our natural leaning towards sin. Sin often feels good, and that is why we find it hard to stop doing it; but it leaves a nasty taste in our mouths because it always causes problems, hurting ourselves and others. We need to make a decision to want to stop doing anything that hurts God, and have an ongoing desire to become pure and holy like Jesus. Purity and holiness is not a boring lifestyle. If you picture those words as creating a life full of religion and

serious, weird intensity, then you need to renew your mind. Now picture someone full of life, happy and passionate, having a blast of an adventure with God, with a mischievous look on their face and a look of being alive in their eyes.

It is an awesome way to live life! It is the only way to live life in all its fullness.

But now you yourselves are to put off all these: anger, wrath, malice, blasphemy, filthy language out of your mouth.

Do not lie to one another, since you have put off the old man with his deeds....

Therefore, as the elect of God, holy and beloved, put on tender mercies, kindness, humility, meekness, longsuffering; bearing with one another, and forgiving one another, if anyone has a complaint against another; even as Christ forgave you, so you also must do.

But above all these things put on love, which is the bond of perfection.

Colossians 3:8–9;12–14

It does not happen overnight, but is a process as we allow God to transform us. It can be frustrating seeing areas in our lives not changing, despite our desire for them to do so, but we have to know that everything is possible, and we just have to keep pressing in, not striving, and knowing God's power in our lives. Even Paul said, 'For what I will to do, that I do not practice, but what I hate, that I do' (Romans 7:15b). But that is not an excuse to give up!

The commandments

There are some commandments that are essential to know, in trying to love God. Loving God leads to life, and loving God is through obedience. Loving God is not some warm feeling that you feel in a worship time, but the decisions that you make which honour God. The commandments are not a list of rules that God asks us to obey before He will accept us; they are a list of things that are wisdom —for living free to know real life. If we approach them with a religious attitude, ready to feel condemned, then we will end up having a relationship with Jesus that is all rules —trying to earn our salvation, and empty of life and passion. Rules without a live relationship kill passion. Jesus said, "He who has My commandments and keeps them, it is he who loves Me." (See John 14:21)

So what are the commandments of God? The Ten Commandments are written in Exodus 20.

1. You shall have no other gods before Me.
2. You shall not make for yourself a carved image…you shall not bow down to them nor serve them….
3. You shall not take the name of the LORD your God in vain….
4. Remember the Sabbath day, to keep it holy….
5. Honour your father and your mother….
6. You shall not murder.
7. You shall not commit adultery.
8. You shall not steal.
9. You shall not bear false witness against your neighbour.
10. You shall not covet….

Jesus sums up the commandments by saying:

"'…you shall love the LORD your God with all your heart, with all your soul, with all your mind and with all your strength. This is the first commandment.

"And the second, like it, is this: 'You shall love your neighbour as yourself.'"

Mark 12:30b

This is fairly amazing stuff! This is the journey that we are all on; to learn to love Jesus and others as much as we love ourselves. If at this point you are thinking that you do not even like yourself, so that won't be a problem, hang on there! We can measure how much we care about ourselves by how much time, energy and money we use to resource ourselves. That helps us understand where we are trying to go. Oh, and if God loves you to the point of giving up His life to give you yours, it is insulting to God to not love yourself.

Loving yourself and self esteem

This is a huge issue, but I want to touch on it briefly. Before we meet Jesus, our self esteem is usually formed in a variety of ways. We develop opinions about ourselves based on the following:

1. What other people have said to us (especially people in authority, like parents, teachers and so on);
2. Our successes and failures (the obvious ones, and the less obvious ones);
3. Our own comparisons with peers, and people presented in the media;
4. Our status in life (family, material possessions, job, etc.)

The good news is that that is not the way to measure yourself, nor is it now the real source of our self-esteem. God looks at you and sees who you really are, and He loves you. He believes in you, and wants to reveal the lies that your subconscious has believed over the years —and to tell you the truth about who you really are. You are not necessarily who people have said you are. You are not a waste of time, stupid, likely to fail at everything, etc. If that kind of stuff has entered into your mind, you need to identify it, and allow God's truth to set you free.

That is why many people change careers when they meet Jesus; they realize that they are able to do things that they never knew were possible, because previously they had listened to lies that had entrapped them. They realise that God wants them to be successful —and He has equipped them to do it. The only place to get our self esteem from is the Bible and all that God says about us.

Our relationships with others

In many cases, as we realize how messed up our minds are with a wrong understanding of who we are and our value, it becomes obvious that we need to learn to speak the truth (with love and kindness) to each other. God put us together as a family so that we can encourage each other. We can learn to speak encouragement to each other and spur one other on to good things. One skill the Holy Spirit teaches us is to 'look for the gold' in everyone. Everyone has some great things about them, and we need to retrain our minds to look for the great stuff, rather than whining about the things that irritate us about them. It is an honour to build people up.

Jesus says to His disciples in Mark 8:34, "Whoever desires to come after Me, let him deny himself, and take up his cross, and follow Me...." As we look at Jesus, we discover that the more we lay down our own interests and selfish purposes at the foot of the cross, the more freedom and life we will know.

We do not wait until other people have encouraged us before we encourage them. Go for it first, without prompting, and 'love without ceasing'. Jesus says, "A new commandment I give to you, that you love one another; as I have loved you, that you also love one another" (John 13:34).

Messing up

It is at this point that it is quite useful to see and understand the whole thing about messing up. The whole 'being friends with Jesus thing' can become a little confusing for us when we know just how bad we can feel over the stuff we have done wrong, stuff we are still doing wrong, and stuff we feel like we will never be able to stop doing wrong. The Bible uses the word 'sin' to describe the stuff that we do that is wrong and hurts others, ourselves and God. The good news is that Jesus forgives us, and that is why He died on the cross in the first place. He needed to die for us because God, the Maker of the world, the holy One, who is perfect and who is love, wants to have a relationship with us, but a holy God cannot be in the presence of sin. Jesus died instead of us, so that we can choose to accept His forgiveness. At the point where we decide to become a Christian (a disciple of Jesus), we get to accept His complete forgiveness, so that God does not even see our sin all over us. When God looks at us He sees us wearing a garment of salvation and a cloak of righteousness. (See Isaiah 61:10.) Jesus bought us that cloak for the price of His blood. Have I lost you here?

A brand new start

It may help to picture this scene that I love to play in my mind a lot. Come with me if you can. Picture all you have done wrong; all the things you would be so embarrassed if people found out you had done; all the thoughts, feelings, actions, nasty things you have said and done. Picture them all kind of written over you, like the worst possible video clips in a strange version of 'This is your Life', and then in your mind begin to walk towards God. Now as you begin to feel embarrassed or ashamed, look towards Jesus and see Him carrying a huge white, shiny cloak. You kneel down and say, 'Yes, Jesus, I believe you died and can wash away all my sin and give me a brand new start. I'm sorry, God, for messing up, sorry for hurting you, sorry for hurting others, sorry for ignoring you and living without you. I want to do life your way, with you at the centre.'

Then see Jesus come and put that shiny, gleaming new cloak around you. As He does, all the guilt of the past mess ups leaves you, and you feel really clean and pure in the depths of your being. It is not like a brain thing, it is in the middle of your being, the place where only you see yourself and others do not even know you. Jesus puts His arm around you and grins at you. You feel this overwhelming sense of love, and relief. You can see the love in His eyes. By the way, I do not know what He looks like (apart from the vision of Him described by John in the Book of Revelation), but I can picture eyes that totally know me and love me, sort of piercing into my heart. Then as He holds you, you walk together confidently to the Father, who sits on this huge white throne, with hordes of angels singing. It is awesome, but you are not scared; wowed, but not frightened, because you know that you are accepted; you are forgiven. There is nothing hidden about you any more. It is a new start.

How was that? Some people find that easy to picture, and some think we are on another planet when I talk like that. That's OK!

What is this blood thing?

You see it is really important to understand how Jesus could do that for us. God made the whole world and put into this world a system where specific blood was the only thing that brings forgiveness. It seems so odd to us who don't think like that now, but blood is the thing that represents life, doesn't it? It is blood that carries life to every cell in our body. So we know really that blood is a significant thing. God wrote it into the way the world works, and God does not change His mind. In Old Testament times, every time that someone messed up, they had to sacrifice animals —different sizes, in proportion to the different kinds of sin It was a complicated system, with different animals and grain for different sins, committed by different people. For example, if a high priest had sinned, he had to offer an unblemished bull; and another person had to offer a male goat or male lamb without blemish. If they were extremely poor, they could offer two young turtledoves or two young pigeons. Then Jesus died, and He was totally sinless and perfect —and now His blood is to be used instead of all the animals, and, as it says in the Bible,

> ...knowing that you were not redeemed with corruptible things, like silver or gold, from your aimless conduct received from tradition from your fathers, but with the precious blood of Christ, as of a lamb without blemish and without spot.
>
> *1 Peter 1:18*

How cool is that? Jesus was the last lamb. The problem is that most people do not understand that this blood thing is written into the order of the world. It is non negotiable. So they cannot understand why they feel guilty, and they either try to numb guilt somehow, or they live feeling pretty bad. But Jesus has the answer. We just have to ask Him to forgive us and set us free.

I do recognise that the whole blood thing sounds odd. But if you put it into modern terms it makes so much sense. So come with me a moment and try this.

Let us think about cars and roads. When roads for cars were built or adapted, a system was designed to ensure as much safety as possible for the drivers, passengers and pedestrians. We are all comfortable and familiar with that system, and we happily adapt to different systems when we travel overseas and hire cars. We either drive on the left or the right, according to the country. People who know how to drive cars and have passed their driving test – and could even be top class racing car drivers – would still get into serious problems if they drove on the wrong side of the road. They could defend their argument using perfect, intelligent language; they could prove their incredible driving skills; but at the end of the day there are rules there that have been invented for good reasons, and the whole driving experience is best if the rules are stuck to. That makes sense, doesn't it? It is the same with the system God set up, that says the blood of Jesus is the only way to receive forgiveness. It is the rule, and that's that! What an awesome rule too; a relationship which brings freedom and life.

Being thankful —which brings life!
A skill that especially we seem to struggle with in many modern societies is the ability to be thankful in every situation —to keep a heart of praise, despite difficulties and problems. The thing is that to live that way is a *decision* that can change your life. It is so simple, and yet so powerful.

Rejoice in the Lord always. Again I will say, rejoice!
Philippians 4:4

Be anxious for nothing, but in everything by prayer and supplication, with thanksgiving, let your requests be made known to God....
Philippians 4:6

Let us come before His presence
with thanksgiving
Psalm 95:2a

There is always so much to thank God for, and when we keep our hearts grateful, we keep our eyes on Him. As we keep our eyes on Him, we are focusing on life, truth, reality, freedom and all that is good, and we can know more of His power released in our hearts. If we are always dwelling on what we lack, or our problems, then we will live in a place of lack, need, and ultimately depression. Practise the skill of being thankful.

What about difficult times?
Difficult times do still come to those of us who follow Jesus, and we are not meant to put on a brave face and pretend that we are feeling great and experiencing no pain. It is good to be able to share with people how hard things are, and enjoy their support and encouragement. It is also awesome to learn to 'run into' God as a 'strong fortress'. He is there for us to turn to, connect with, and pour out our emotion to. We need to learn to allow Him to shelter us, heal us, restore us, and give us new strength. Praise and thanksgiving are keys to getting through hard times, even if they seem somewhat inappropriate! Paul and Silas were singing praise to God while in prison.

> But at midnight Paul and Silas were praying and singing hymns to God, and the prisoners were listening to them.
> *Acts 16:25*

They did not deserve to be in prison, and they had every reason to feel sorry for themselves and be miserable. Self pity would have been a blockage to faith. In fact, they were so full of the Holy Spirit, and so full of faith, that they could pray and sing to God. It is almost impossible to believe God for a miracle, keep your eyes fixed on Him, and trust Him when you are feeling sorry for yourself! No matter what situation you are facing, when you start to thank God for the blessings that are in your life, you will begin to have a different perspective.

When the difficulties do come in life, with Jesus they look so different. Even the worst situations become opportunities for us to grow in determination and wisdom. Every experience we get through can be used to help others. Bad times can create a passion in us to overcome. We still feel grief, pain, sadness, and other such emotions, but we know that they will not overwhelm us, as we have the Creator of the world holding us and walking with us. We walk through the 'valley of the shadow of death' as it is described in Psalm 23; we do not have to camp there!

In conclusion

With Jesus —nothing is impossible. Keep your eyes on Him, and keep seeking Him first. Live a life of adventure and faith. Do everything to bring Him pleasure, and enjoy knowing His unconditional, awesome and overwhelming love. Have a blast!